Don't Leave Home Without It

A primer on the infilling of the Holy Spirit

Delron Shirley

©2019

Table of Contents

This teaching manual is intended for personal study; however, the author encourages all students to also become teachers and to share the truths from this text with others. However, copying the text itself without permission from the author is considered plagiarism which is punishable by law. To obtain permission to quote material from this book, please contact:

Delron Shirley
3210 Cathedral Spires Dr.
Colorado Springs, CO 80904
719-685-9999
www.teachallnationsmission.com
teachallnations@msn.com

The Holy Spirit – A Key Element in Jesus' Life

When Jesus' disciples saw Him praying, they realized that there was something really different about the way He prayed; so they asked Him to let them in on His secret. (Luke 11:1) He began with a simple explanation of the substance of an effectual prayer – what we know of today as the Lord's Prayer. (Luke 11:2-4) He then turned to the relationship with the Heavenly Father that is necessary to activate an efficacious prayer life – His comparison between the resistant neighbor who was reluctant to get up and help his friend who had a need at midnight and the father who readily gives good gifts to his son. (Luke 11:5-12) But He concluded His answer with an unexpected element – the promise that the Heavenly Father will give the Holy Spirit to those of us who ask. (Luke 11:13) In essence, Jesus knew that effective praying requires three necessary ingredients – content (the aspects of the Lord's Prayer), connection (a father-son relationship with God), and counsel (the direction of the Holy Spirit).

Certainly, the middle element (the personal connection with the Heavenly Father) was the most important aspect of Jesus' prayer life; however, the counsel of the Holy Spirit was another unique and necessary ingredient. Actually, the Holy Spirit had been involved in the earthly life of Jesus from before His birth. It was the Holy Spirit who overshadowed the Virgin Mary to cause her to conceive through the divine seed of God. (Matthew 1:20) As a child, Jesus grew spiritually strong. (Luke 2:40) But it was at the Jordan River where He came strongly under the direction of the Holy Spirit and was led – or as Mark describes the event, was driven – into the wilderness by the Holy Spirit. (Luke 4:1, Mark 1:12) There He fasted forty days and then confronted the devil himself nose-to-nose and won. The scriptures record that after this experience, Jesus returned to civilization in an even greater relationship with the Holy Spirit; He was empowered by the Spirit. (Luke 4:14) In His very first sermon, Jesus testified that the power of His ministry was in the relationship He had with the Holy Spirit. (Luke 4: 18-19) This statement was in accordance with the Old Testament prophecies concerning the Holy Spirit's ministry in the life of the coming Messiah. (Isaiah 11:2, 61:1) He confirmed that the source of His ability to do miraculous acts was the Holy Spirit. (Matthew 12:28) In fact, a careful study of the scriptures will reveal that it was the presence of the Holy Spirit with Jesus that made Him different. The Holy Spirit worked through Jesus right up through the end of His earthly ministry (Acts 10:38), at the resurrection (Romans 8:11), and even until the day in which He was taken up (Acts 1:2).

Since this involvement by the Holy Spirit was of such significance in His own life, Jesus promised that the relationship that He had with the Holy Spirit was something that He would share with His disciples. (John 14:16-17) He even commanded that His disciples not try to minister until they had received that relationship. (Luke 24:49) Jesus took the very last occasion He had with the disciples prior to His arrest and crucifixion to emphasize how important it was that they receive the Holy Spirit and to explain how the Holy Spirit would work for and through the believers. (John 14:16 - 16:15) Jesus also took the last minutes He had with the disciples just before His ascension into heaven to again emphasize to the disciples their need for the Holy Spirit. (Acts 1:4-5, 8)

The Holy Spirit - A Promise to Believers

John the Baptist had promised that Jesus would baptize His followers in the Holy Spirit. (Matthew 3:11, Mark 1:8, Luke 3:16, John 1:33, Acts 1:5) Certainly the disciples anticipated this baptism in the Holy Spirit every day during their three years with Jesus. They did, indeed, experience the supernatural on a regular basis as they lived and traveled with the Master. They saw multitudes fed with only a handful of fish and bread (Matthew 14:20), they witnessed innumerable healings (Matthew 4:23) and deliverances (Mark 1:27), they drank wine that had been transformed from clear water (John 2:9), they marveled as storms at sea quieted at His command (Mark 4:39), they trembled as Jesus walked on water and even invited them to join Him (Matthew 14:28), they had even seen the dead raised to life again (John 11:44); but they never experienced the fulfillment of the promise to be baptized in the Holy Spirit. I can imagine that they must have doubted Jesus' promise concerning being baptized in the Holy Spirit when they saw their Master taken in arrest and eventually executed without giving them the Holy Spirit. I'm certain that they were thrilled when Jesus renewed this promise after His resurrection. (Acts 1:5) In these last moments with their Master before He departed this earthly realm, He once again renewed the promise and commanded them that they wait to receive this all-important impetus for their lives and ministry. (Acts 1:4-5)

The fulfillment of this divine promise finally came on the Day of Pentecost – just a matter of days after Jesus' ascension back to the Father. Pentecost was the Jewish festival with two significant aspects. Spiritually, it commemorated the giving of the Old Testament law; physically, it celebrated the harvest. With this in mind, it is easy to see why the Lord wanted to wait until Pentecost to send the Holy Spirit. The giving of the Holy Spirit brought believers into a new relationship with God so that the Law became internalized in their hearts rather than codified on tablets of stone and in ink-filled books. (Jeremiah 31:33-34, Hebrews 8:10-11) Additionally, the Holy Spirit is the agent of bringing in the spiritual harvest of souls that parallels the ingathering of the physical fruit of the earth. This is the reason why as soon as Jesus had told the disciples that they were to be His envoys in the world in the same manner that He was the Father's representative, He breathed on them and commanded that they receive Holy Spirit. (John 20:22) It was for the same reason that He commanded that they not try to go out and fulfill the Great Commission until they first tarried in Jerusalem for the outpouring of the Spirit. (Luke 24:49) Additionally, this is the exact motivation for His last words to them – that they were to receive power after that the Holy Ghost is come upon them, equipping them to take the message of salvation to the vary ends of the earth. (Acts 1:8) Jesus repeatedly told the disciples that they were to go out and preach the gospel around the world; yet, He suddenly jerked them back from that task by telling them that they could not do so until after they had received the promise of the Father – the promise that was fulfilled on the Day of Pentecost. (Luke 24:49, Act 1:4) He wanted to use this day to give a "jumpstart" to the spread of the gospel around the world. In the giving of the Great Commission as it is recorded in Luke 24:46-49, Jesus told the disciples that they would be witnesses to all the nations and that this witness would begin from Jerusalem. He then went on to direct them to tarry in Jerusalem until they would receive a supernatural gift from their heavenly Father.

In his second volume – the book of Acts – Luke told us the rest of the story when he recorded that on the day of Pentecost there were devout men from every nation under heaven gathered in Jerusalem for the celebration. (Acts 2:5) When the Holy Spirit was poured out on the believers who had gathered in the Upper Room, they were supernaturally given the ability to speak in the languages of all these visitors. The result was that men and women from all the foreign lands in addition to the local residents turned to Jesus that one day. It is only logical to assume that these visitors returned to their own homes once the festival was over. They took with them the message of salvation that they had heard on the Day of Pentecost. In essence, Jesus used the delay in filling the believers with the Holy Spirit as a way of inaugurating their mission of taking the gospel to the nations. As He had said, they began in Jerusalem, but they also instantly impacted the whole world. The miracle of Pentecost was not simply that there were supernatural manifestations of wind, fire, and tongues (Acts 2:2-4), that on one day the gospel was preached to men from every nation under heaven (Acts 2:5), or that three thousand responded to the message (Acts 2:41). It was that men were emboldened and empowered to stand up and preach the gospel. (Acts 2:14) Jesus had promised that it would be through physical manifestations of the presence of the Holy Spirit in the demonstration of signs and wonders that the disciples would be able to fulfill the Great Commission. (Mark 16:17-18) The record of those early Christians is that it was through Pentecostal manifestations that they were able to accomplish all they did to further the kingdom. (Romans 15:19, Hebrews 2:4) Not only is the work of the Holy Spirit in bringing in the harvest a historical reality, it is also a prophetic certainty, "The Spirit and the bride say, Come." (Revelation 22:17)

Have you ever noticed that the twelve men who followed Jesus were almost always called "disciples" in the gospels, but became "apostles" in the book of Acts? This name change signified the radical change that occurred in their lives when they were empowered by the Holy Spirit on the Day of Pentecost. Because of the power that the disciples received when they were filled with the Holy Spirit on the Day of Pentecost, the number of believers multiplied from one hundred twenty to three thousand in a single day – a twenty-five thousand percent increase! (Acts 1:15, Acts 2:41) The phenomenal outpouring of the Holy Spirit totally revolutionized the lives of the disciples – transforming them into radically different people. The men who only a few days before cowardly denied knowing Jesus (Mark 14:72) and forsook Him and hid behind locked doors rather than risk being accused with Him (Matthew 26:56, Mark 14:50, John 20:19) suddenly became fearless defenders of the faith (Acts 5:27-32). The total lives of the believers were revolutionized by this new relationship with the Holy Spirit. They became intensely interested in studying the Bible (Acts 2:42), they loved the fellowship of believers (Acts 2:46), they began to manifest supernatural signs and wonders (Acts 2:43), they were filled with joy (Acts 2:46), they had a great devotion to prayer and worship (Acts 2:47), they became soul winners (Acts 2:47), and they generously shared with those in need (Acts 2:44-45).

As phenomenal as that may seem, the report of what happened when the Spirit was poured out in Ephesus is even more earthshaking – the church grew from just twelve believers until it had infected all of Asia in just two years. (Acts 19:7-10) Saul of Tarsus was transformed into the Apostle Paul when he had a life-changing encounter on the road to Damascus and was filled with the Holy Spirit a few days later. (Acts 9:17) The result of this spiritual infilling was that he was able to fully preach the Gospel from Jerusalem all the way to Central Greece (Romans 15:19) and to attest that there was no more place that had not been penetrated with his ministry (Romans 15:23). Additionally, he had such a powerful ministry in the Turkish city of Ephesus that the temple to Diana (one of the Seven Wonders of the Ancient World that drew devotees from all over the world) almost went into bankruptcy due to the loss of worshippers. (Acts 19:27) He later indicated that the key to his success in the ministry that was to follow was his relationship with the Holy Spirit. (Romans 15:19, I Corinthians 2:4, I Thessalonians 1:5) Of course, this continued outpouring of the Spirit was of no surprise since Peter had promised it in his very first sermon on the Day of Pentecost, "I will pour out of my Spirit upon all flesh...For the promise is unto you, and to your children, and to all that are afar off, even as many as the Lord our God shall call." (Acts 2:17-39)

Matthew 24:14 promises that in the last days the gospel of the kingdom will be preached in all the nations of the world. A parallel promise concerning the end time is that the Holy Spirit will be poured out upon all flesh. (Joel 2:28, Acts 2:17) As they say – it shouldn't take a rocket scientist to see the connection. For the gospel to penetrate the nations today as it did in the days of the early church, the contemporary church needs the same power that those first-century believers had – the power of Pentecost. If the presence and power of the Holy Spirit were important enough to the apostles that Jesus would command them to receive them, the command is equally as strong for us. Paul expressed that it is still a command of God when he penned the words of Ephesians 5:18, "Be filled with the Spirit."

In our spiritual lives, just as in Jesus' earthly life, we have differing levels of relationships with the Holy Spirit. At the time we become believers, we receive the Holy Spirit. Jesus described this to Nicodemus who came secretly to Him at night to ask about entering the kingdom of Heaven. (John 3:5-8) Paul furthered this discussion with the statement that we are not associated with Christ unless we have received the Holy Spirit. (Romans 8:9) In an illustration of this level of relationship with the Holy Spirit, Paul used the figure of drinking in the Spirit. (I

10

Corinthians 12:13) Jesus characterized this relationship as a breath when He ministered to His disciples during that last forty days of fellowship prior to his return to the Father. (John 20:22) This experience of receiving the Holy Spirit through the breath of Jesus was God's deliberate attempt to show us the parallel between the infusion of life at the spiritual rebirth and the original infusion of life when God the Father breathed into the lifeless model of man He had fashioned from the dust of the earth. (Genesis 2:7) Both of these illustrations set the stage for an understanding of the next level of relationship we are to enter into with the Holy Spirit: a drink is to be contrasted with the gushing of rivers and a breath is to be compared to a rushing mighty wind. Jesus Himself told us that the Spirit that we received as a drink could, and should, erupt out of us as rivers of living water. (John 7:38-39) Acts records for us how that simple breath of the Holy Spirit became a gale-force blast on the Day of Pentecost. (Acts 2:1-4) This intensified relationship with the Holy Spirit was called the baptism in the Holy Spirit.

Many times, there is confusion as to the difference between the baptism in the Holy Spirit and the fact that we received the Holy Spirit when we were born again. During His conversation with the disciples over the Last Supper, Jesus made if perfectly clear that at salvation the entire Trinity – Father, Son, and Holy Spirit – would take up residence in the lives of all believers. (John 14:23) Therefore, the Holy Spirit has been part of each of our lives since the instant that we punctuated "the sinner's prayer" with the closing "Amen." However, there is a difference – not in the presence of the Holy Spirit in our lives – but in the quantity and direction of His operation in us when we are baptized in the Holy Spirit.

Speaking of our salvation Paul described the Holy Spirit's presence as taking a drink. (I Corinthians 12:13) Notice that the movement is inward and the quantity is limited to as much as we can consume. On the other hand, Jesus described the baptism in the Holy Spirit as rivers of living water flowing out of us. (John 7:38-39) Here the movement is outward and the quantity is unlimited – think of the raging Colorado, the flowing Nile, the flooding Mississippi, the gushing Amazon, the roaring Columbia, the surging Niagara, and the rolling Danube all combined. The important thing to understand here is that the baptism of the Holy Spirit is God's way of releasing what He put in us at salvation. Like the seed that goes into the ground as a single kernel and comes back out of the ground thirty, sixty, or a hundred times more abundant (John 12:24, Mark 4:8), the Holy Spirit is released to do a more abundant outward work to bless others after He has done His internal work to bless our lives.

The Holy Spirit – The Person of God Present with Us

It is of utmost importance that we remember that Jesus referred to the Holy Spirit in personal terms – as an individual rather than as an influence or substance. Unfortunately, many people today see Him as an influence rather than a person with whom we are to develop a relationship. If we truly understood the Holy Spirit as He is portrayed in the scriptures, we would readily see Him as a person – not just an influence or doctrine. He is God with all the qualities and characteristics of the Father and Jesus. The Holy Spirit is not just an influence, an anointing, a power, a mystery, or an experience – He is a divine person to be loved, revered, and welcomed just as we would Jesus Himself. Until we come to know the person and personality of the Holy Spirit, we are going to miss the most important factor that we have available to us in fulfilling our commission in the world today.

One of the first truths that we need to realize about the person of the Holy Spirit is that He is equal and co-existing with the Father and Jesus. Jesus Himself told the original disciples to recognize Him as equal when baptizing new believers into the church. (Matthew 28:19) The Apostle Paul recognized the co-existing quality of the Holy Spirit when he addressed the Corinthian church. (II Corinthians 13:14) Even though we will come to know the Holy Spirit as a person and as a friend on an individual level, it is of ultimate importance that we never allow ourselves to see Him as any bit less than God Himself. He must always be reverenced, respected, and honored on an equal basis as God the Father or God the Son.

As a person, rather than a force or influence, the Holy Spirit is affected by the way we relate to Him and act toward Him. We can grieve Him (Ephesians 4:30) and resist Him (Acts 7:51). It is possible to quench His relationship with us. (I Thessalonians 5:19) Isaiah claims that our rebelliousness is vexing to the Holy Spirit. (verse 63:10) The history of the early church records that one couple attempted to lie to the Holy Spirit. (Acts 5:3) Jesus warned that some people can even blaspheme the Holy Spirit. (Mark 3:29) King David realized that his sins could separate him from the presence and fellowship of the Holy Spirit. (Psalm 51:11) But above all the negative relationships that can develop, it is important to focus on the fact that we can develop a positive communion with Him. (II Corinthians 13:14)

The Bible gives us a number of descriptive terms to help us recognize how the Holy Spirit wants to relate to us and help us. He is called the Spirit of Christ (Romans 8:9) and the Spirit of God (Genesis 1:2). Isaiah listed the seven-fold nature of the Holy Spirit mentioned in Revelation 3:1 in his prophecy concerning how the Holy Spirit was to anoint Jesus. (Isaiah 11:2) Jesus spoke of the Holy Spirit as the spirit of truth. (John 14:17) Paul similarly referred to him as the spirit of wisdom and revelation. (Ephesians 1:17) This is an important characteristic because it determines that He will always relate to us truthfully and will demand the same from us. In a world with so much deception and lying, it is comforting to know that there is a spirit of truth desiring fellowship with us. Jesus continued that this spirit of truth would guide us into all truth. (John 16:13) This means that He will reveal to us the wonderful truths of God and that He will direct us as we enter into these revelations. This is a very encouraging assurance since truth without guidance can be dangerous. Just knowing truth is not enough; we must be expertly guided into how to relate to it and use it wisely. Perhaps that is why the Holy Spirit is also called a teacher (Luke 12:12) and a comforter (John 14:26). The Holy Spirit should be an ever-welcomed assistant in our lives in that He is our source of divine power (Acts 1:8) and guidance (Romans 8:14), plus the very one who establishes our relation to God (Romans 8:15). Jesus saw the Holy Spirit as a necessity for the believer to the point that He said that it was better for Him (Jesus) to go away so that the Holy Spirit could come into His full place (John 16:7), resulting in the believers' being able to do even greater works than Jesus Himself did (John 14:12).

If we were to begin to enumerate the functions of the Holy Spirit, we would find an almost limitless agenda. But let's list just a few:

He is a creator. (Genesis 1:2)
He is the one who convicts. (John 16:7-8)
He is the seal of our redemption. (Ephesians 1:13)
He is our enabler. (Zechariah 4:6)
He is our comforter. (John 16:7)
He is our revealer of truth. (John 16:13)
He is a builder. (Ephesians 2:20-22)
He is our source of love. (Romans 5:5)
He is our source of joy. (Romans 14:17)
He is our judge or the one who reproves us. (John 16:8)
He is our earnest or the guarantee of our spiritual rights. (II Corinthians 1:22)
He is our prayer instructor. (Romans 8:26-28)
He is our link to divine knowledge. (I Corinthians 2:9-11)
He is the agent of our new birth. (John 3:5)
He is our source of quickening life. (Romans 8:9-11)
He is the inspirer of the scriptures. (II Peter 1:21)
He is the instructor of spiritual truths. (I Corinthians 2:13)
He is the one who indwells believers. (I Corinthians 6:19-20)

He is our sanctifier. (I Peter 1:2)

He is our avenue to hope. (Galatians 5:5)

He is our link to the free gifts of God. (I Corinthians 2:12)

He is the one who changes us from glory to glory. (II Corinthians 3:18)

He is the one who provides access to the Father. (Ephesians 2:18)

He is the one who calls men to Jesus. (Revelation 22:17)

He is the one who warns us of demonic deception. (I Timothy 4:1)

He is the one who helps us keep the things of God. (II Timothy 1:14)

He is the one who renews us. (Titus 3:5)

He is the one who confirms our witness. (Hebrews 2:4)

He is the one who gives us a foretaste of heaven. (Hebrews 6:4)

He is the one who empowers and enlightens our preaching. (I Peter 1:12)

He is our source of faith building. (Jude 20)

He is our source of protection. (Isaiah 59:19)

He is the one who communicates victory to the churches. (Revelation 2:7)

He is the one who eliminates doubt. (Acts 11:12)

He is the one who forewarns us. (Acts 20:23)

He is the one who forbids our wrong directions. (Acts 16:6)

He is the one who separates those chosen for divine service. (Acts 13:2)

The Holy Spirit bears all the qualities and characteristics of deity; He is God! (I John 5:7) He is omnipotent. (Zechariah 4:6) He is omniscient. (I Corinthians 2:10) He is omnipresent. (Psalms 139:7-10)

He is eternal. (Hebrews 9:14) This means that God Himself is living with and in us when we come to know the Holy Spirit. We are not feeling just an influence or having an experience; we are entering into a personal relationship with God Himself. Through knowing the Holy Spirit, we come to prove wrong the Babylonian astrologers who said that the spirit of God does not dwell with men. (Daniel 2:11) Throughout the Old Testament period, men knew the Holy Spirit in a limited way. They would experience His presence and anointing on special occasions and then the Holy Spirit's presence would depart from them. (Numbers 11:25; Judges 3:9-10, 6:34, 11:29, 15:14; I Samuel 16:13) Samson was a great example of this pattern of living. He would receive a visitation of the Spirit of God for a specific function in his struggle against the enemies of God and Israel; yet, as soon as the conflict was over, he would return to his natural, carnal lifestyle. The book of Judges describes the Holy Spirit almost as a yo-yo bouncing up and down upon the man Samson. (verses 13:25, 14:6, 19, 15:14) Between these visitations of the divine Spirit, Samson's life showed no qualities of a spiritual nature at all; he was just as likely to be found in bed with a harlot as to be about anything else. (verse 16:1) This picture changes in the New Testament. First, we find that the Holy Spirit came to Jesus in a new dimension which none of the Old Testament saints experienced. John testifies that he saw the Holy Spirit rest and remain upon Jesus. (John 1:32-33) The key thought here is that the Holy Spirit remained upon Jesus. He did not just appear for a short visit and then depart, as had been the Old Testament pattern. John further testified that the impartation of the Holy Spirit to Jesus was without measure. (John 3:34) This means that the totality of the Holy Spirit was with our Lord. He did not just receive the power of the Holy Spirit or the wisdom of the Spirit or any other quality or a few gifts from the Holy Spirit; He received the totality of who the Holy Spirit is and what He possesses – Jesus received the Holy Spirit Himself!

There was never any indication that this powerful relationship with the Spirit of God was limited to just the New Testament era. In fact, the scriptures clearly state that this promise is to anyone who will receive it. (Acts 2:39) The scriptures give us some definite instructions as to how to enter into this deeper relationship with the Holy Spirit. The most obvious way to enter into a deeper relationship with the Holy Spirit is to simply ask. (Luke 11:13) Some people expect God to give them gifts without their anticipating them; occasionally this does happen, but the biblical pattern is that we should ask for what we want from God. In fact, the Apostle Paul tells us to intensely desire the benefits of this deeper relationship with the Holy Spirit. (I Corinthians 12:31, 14:1) In the asking, we should ask with simple trust and confidence just like we would ask our earthly parents for our daily needs. (Luke 11:11-13) We should receive without fear. (II Timothy 1:7) We should receive in faith. (Galatians 3:2) We should receive through prayer. (Jude 20) We should receive with love. (I Corinthians 13:1-3) We can receive through the laying on of hands. (Deuteronomy 34:8-9, Acts 9:17, I Timothy 4:14, II Timothy 1:6) We can receive a new relationship with the Holy Spirit by learning the truth about spiritual things. (I Corinthians 12:1) We must also activate the gifts by beginning to function in them by faith. (I Timothy 4:14) The one thing to remember about the baptism in the Holy Spirit is that similar to the baptism in water, the recipient must willingly submit to the baptizer (Jesus) to be submerged in the Holy Spirit and to be filled with His presence. (Acts 1:5)

Living in this deeper relationship with the Holy Spirit opens up many new spiritual dimensions to us. One of these is the use of the gifts of the Holy Spirit that Paul enumerated in I Corinthians chapter twelve. I personally prefer to call these our tools of ministry. Just as a carpenter needs his hammer and a plumber needs his wrench, we must have the gifts – or tools – of the Holy Spirit to accomplish the tasks that Christ left us to do: to evangelize and disciple the world (Mark 16:15-16, Matthew 28:18-20) and to be His representatives during His absence (Luke 19:13). These various gifts – which we will study in detail a little later on – are distributed to the variety of individuals in the Body of Christ so that they can make their best contribution to the total operation of the church. Just as we would not give a word processor to the carpenter or a hammer to the secretary, the Holy Spirit in His wisdom gives each person the gift that he needs most to fulfill the job he is to complete in the church. When each person finds his proper place and uses his proper tool, the church as a whole grows and prospers. (I Corinthians 12:7, 11) But more important than the gifts are the motives through which the gifts are operated. Both the Apostle Paul and the Apostle Peter addressed this issue. (Romans 12: 4-21, I Peter 4:10-11) In a word, Paul summarized the proper motivation as love. (I Corinthians 12:31 - 14:1) In another place Paul described love as walking or living in the Spirit (Galatians 5: 16-18), and he continued to give a multifaceted description of the fruit of such a spiritual walk or life (Galatians 5:22-23).

This relationship with the Holy Spirit as a person and a helper, not just an influence or an anointing, gives the believer a fresh level of victory in his Christian life that can never be obtained otherwise. Even the great Apostle Paul described his Christian life as marked by one defeat after another until he moved into this new fellowship with the divine Comforter. (Romans 7:14-25) When he allowed the Holy Spirit to become an integral part of his life, he entered into victory in his Christian life. (Romans 8:1-17, 26-28)

The Holy Spirit – A Gift to Receive

In each of the accounts in the book of Acts of the believers' encounters with the Holy Spirit, it is immediately apparent that the coming of the Holy Spirit is a separate experience from salvation. The believers in the Upper Room (Acts 2:4) had been followers of Christ during His earthly ministry and had certainly received Him as their Lord, else they would not have gathered in Jerusalem after His death. The believers described in chapter four were converted on the Day of Pentecost and during the following days of evangelism in Jerusalem; yet, they had a separate experience with the Holy Spirit when they gathered for prayer after having been arrested for preaching the gospel. (Acts 4:31) The people of Samaria received salvation under the ministry of Philip yet had not received the power of the Holy Spirit until Peter and John came to pray for them. (Acts 8:14-17) Paul was unquestionably converted on the road to Damascus before he was filled with the Holy Spirit when Ananias visited him in the house on Straight Street. (Acts 9:17) The members of Cornelius' household were apparently already sincerely religious folk and most likely fully accepted the gospel message as Peter ministered to them. (Acts 10:44-46) Even though the disciples at Ephesus were originally baptized under John the Baptist's ministry and knew little of the fulfillment of the prophetic message they had heard him preach, they had to have been believers – either from their previous experience or from the present ministry of Paul – before the apostle would consent to baptize them. (Acts 19:6)

The other pattern that is consistent among these experiences is that each is accompanied by some supernatural sign. In the Upper Room, they all supernaturally spoke in languages they had not learned. The persecuted believers in the prayer huddle began to preach the gospel boldly – perhaps they had supernatural languages, but for sure they used their native language with a new anointing. The gentile converts in Cornelius' courtyard all spoke with unknown tongues as did the disciples in Ephesus. In Samaria, something supernatural happened to the people when they were filled with the Holy Spirit. Although the scriptures do not tell us exactly what it was, we know that it was something different from healings, deliverances from demonic power, and manifestations of divine joy. All these things had happened in the ministry of Philip who first brought the gospel to the city. (Acts 8:6-8) Although Simon the Magician had witnessed all these miraculous moves of God and had been impressed by them enough to become a Christian (Acts 8:13), he was not overwhelmed to the point that he was willing to offer money to receive the ability to make them happen. (Acts 8:18) Something else – something dramatic – occurred when the people were filled with the Spirit – something so out of the ordinary that he felt he must have the power to recreate it in his magic show! Most Bible scholars – even the very liberal ones – concede that this supernatural manifestation must have been the speaking in unknown tongues. In the case of Saul of Tarsus, we have no record that he spoke in tongues on the day Ananias laid hands on him; however, we know from his own testimony that he consistently manifested this supernatural enduement in his own personal life. (I Corinthians 14:18)

The conclusion we can draw from this survey of the historical record is that in half of the incidents recorded in Acts (Pentecost, Cornelius' household, Ephesus), there is a definite record that the believers immediately spoke in tongues when they received the baptism in the Holy Spirit. In two of the remaining three incidents (Samaria and Paul), it is likely that they also spoke with tongues as a result of receiving the Holy Spirit into their lives. The one remaining account (the persecuted believers) leaves no reason to doubt that they might also have received this supernatural gift. As a result, we should anticipate that believers who truly receive the fullness of the Holy Spirit should also manifest this divine gift of speaking in unknown tongues.

Why does God use such an unusual manifestation as speaking in unknown tongues to confirm the presence of His Holy Spirit in the lives of His followers? The answer is possibly in the fact that the tongue is the one element of creation over which man seems powerless. The Apostle James gave us a vivid description:

> For in many things we offend all. If any man offend not in word, the same is a perfect man, and able also to bridle the whole body. Behold, we put bits in the horses' mouths, that they may obey us; and we turn about their whole body. Behold also the ships, which though they be so great, and are driven of fierce winds, yet are they turned about with a very small helm, whithersoever the governor listeth. Even so the tongue is a little member, and boasteth great things. Behold, how great a matter a little fire kindleth! And the tongue is a fire, a world of iniquity: so is the tongue among our members, that it defileth the whole body, and setteth on fire the course of nature; and it is set on fire of hell. For every kind of beasts, and of birds, and of serpents, and of things in the sea, is tamed, and hath been tamed of mankind: But the tongue can no man tame; it is an unruly evil, full of deadly poison. (James 3:2-8)

When we allow the Holy Spirit to control our tongues to the point that we speak supernaturally under His inspiration, we have finally come under His complete control! Using this new Spirit-inspired language brings many benefits into the life of the believer. Speaking in tongues is for our personal edification (I Corinthians 14:4), a benefit not only for the individual believer but also for those around him. How can I expect to help anyone else when I'm in the dumps myself?   Isaiah 28:11-12 prophesied that tongues would be a refreshing for the believer, and Romans 8:26-28 teaches us that praying in tongues will empower our prayer life to the point that we will know that everything in our lives will work together for good. Jude says that the use of this gift is a way to build ourselves up on our most holy faith. (Jude 20) This gift serves as a new and effective way to communicate to God in prayer or praise. (I Corinthians 14:2, 14-16, 28) It is important to note that Paul specifically said that he willed – or determined – to pray with the Spirit (in tongues) and that he willed – or determined – to also pray with the mind (in his understanding).   The point is that it is vitally important to pray in the Spirit because the Holy Spirit helps us when we don't know how to pray or what to pray for. Since He is God, He knows the mind of God and, therefore, prays according to the very will and nature of God. When He prays for and through us, we have no doubt that things are going to work out perfectly for us. (Romans 8:26-28) On the other hand, Paul insists that he is going to continue to pray prayers that he intellectually constructs because it is in this deliberate formulation of prayers that we train ourselves to think and speak in accordance with the mind, will, and Word of God. It is just as essential for believers to develop a prayer life in our known language as it is for us to develop the practice of allowing the Holy Spirit to lead us in our prayer. I often say that we must be careful not to put our prayers on "autopilot."

At this point, it might be good to introduce a "disclaimer" since there are those who feel that the whole essence of the Pentecostal message is centered around speaking in tongues. Considering the attention that I have already given to the topic, I can certainly understand their confusion. But let's go back to the list of the events in the book of Acts in which believers were filled with the Holy Spirit and revisit the incident recorded in Acts chapter four. This account reports that the Holy Spirit gave them the power to speak the word of God with boldness. (Acts 4:31) This story does not necessarily say that the believers spoke in tongues, but they did receive an empowered ability to speak in their own language – the element that followed the speaking in tongues on the Day of Pentecost. After the apostles experienced glossolalia (Acts 2:7-11), they then stood up boldly and proclaimed the gospel in their own language (Acts 2:14). The significance of speaking in tongues is that it gets the believer into the proper position to speak boldly and effectively in his own language. Jude says that it builds us in our faith – faith that will result in effective witnessing.

Speaking in tongues is also a benefit for unbelievers because it can be a sign to lead them to salvation. (I Corinthians 14:22) In essence, the gift of tongues is a reversal of the confusion of the languages that occurred at Babel. In Genesis 11:9, God made it impossible for men to understand one another; but in Acts 2:8-11 He gave the apostles a supernatural ability to speak in at least sixteen languages which they had never learned. The result was three thousand conversions in one day. This same miraculous gift has been repeated throughout church history in the lives of such missionaries as the sixteenth-century Catholic pioneer Francis Xavier who is credited with winning thousands of souls in India,

China, and Japan when he preached to them in their native languages without having learned them. Even in my own life, I've seen this miraculous gift in demonstration on several occasions. When a group of English-speaking missionaries from the US and Canada were doing house-to-house visitation in the Dominican Republic, we had national Christians who knew only a very limited amount of English introduce us to the families. When a sick baby in one of the homes was handed to a lady on our team, she began to pray in fluent Spanish – although she didn't know a word of the language. After the prayer, it was impossible to explain to the people why none of us could communicate with them in their language. On another occasion, I took a young man who was still undecided about the gospel to a prayer meeting. During the prayer time, the gentleman seated beside my friend began to pray in tongues. When my friend turned to me and commented that the gentleman must be Italian, I explained that I knew the man and was certain that he was not Italian. My friend explained that his grandparents were from Italy and that he recognized Italian when it was being spoken. When he insisted that the gentleman was speaking in Italian, I explained about the miracle of speaking in tongues. This encounter was enough to convince him that God is real, and he accepted the Lord as his savior that very day! The next purpose for speaking in tongues is to deliver a divine message to the church. Such messages must always be interpreted so that the people can understand the communication. (I Corinthians 14:13, 27) And I have an amazing experience to relate about this phenomenon, but it must wait for the proper time.

Twice, Paul instructed us that we must have a desire for the spiritual gifts. (I Corinthians 12:31, 14:1) He instructed us to actually covet the best gifts – meaning the best ones for our particular callings in life. However, it doesn't matter how much we desire the Spirit-filled life, we simply will not have it without taking the next obvious step – ask for it. Jesus taught us to ask with the same sincerity and simple faith that we would ask our earthly father for a piece of bread and expect that he would give us bread and not a stone. (Luke 11:13) Paul piggybacks on this idea by teaching us that faith is a key factor in receiving this blessing. (Galatians 3:2) There is a biblical pattern of having church leaders lay their hands on those who are seeking to be filled with the Spirit as a form of impartation (Acts 8:17, 18, 19; 9:17; 13:3; 19:6; I Timothy 4:14; II Timothy 1:6); however, not every occurrence required this external act – for example, the household of Cornelius received simply by hearing the preaching of the Word of God (Acts 10:44). The Apostle Paul directed his protégé Timothy that he not passively neglect the gifts of the Holy Spirit (I Timothy 4:14) but instead actively stir them up in his life and ministry (II Timothy 1:6). The apostle also used his own experience to illustrate the necessity to aggressively pursue and activate the Holy Spirit's manifestation when he said that he willed (or determined) to pray in the Spirit on the same level that he disciplined himself to pray in his natural language. (I Corinthians 14:15) Additionally, he encouraged believers not to settle for just an occasional experience with just one manifestation of The Holy Spirit's operation but to seek for multiple expressions of these gifts. (I Corinthians 12:11)

In Matthew 15:21-28, we read the story of a gentile woman who came to Jesus beseeching Him to deliver her daughter who was grievously vexed by demons. After Jesus first replied with a response that seemed to be a rejection, she countered His statement that bread should be given to the children with a persistent argument that even the dogs can eat of the crumbs that fall from the children's table. From this illustration, we can learn a lesson about not settling for less than is our legitimate right. Even though the gentile woman was accustomed to being treated like a dog by her Jewish neighbors, she had come to realize that even dogs have rights – and she claimed hers. As Christians, we are the children of God – not dogs; therefore, we are entitled to the full loaf – not just a few crumbs. Thus, we need to realize that God desires to give us His blessings abundantly. Unfortunately, most of the time we fail to really anticipate what He wants to release into our lives – both physically and spiritually. How often is it that we don't even insist upon the crumbs, much less the whole loaf!

The Holy Spirit - A Gift to Share

Second Corinthians 9:10 says that God supplies on two different levels – seed for sowing and bread for eating. We have already considered the fact that He gives us the Holy Spirit at salvation like a seed and multiplies His work in our lives through the baptism in the Holy Spirit as an abundant harvest. I encourage you enjoy both the seed and the harvest. Take the whole loaf to feed yourself and share with others. And that loaf includes much more than just the ability to speak in tongues. In fact, there is a whole array of supernatural abilities that the Holy Spirit desires to impart to us so that we will have something supernatural to give to the world.

These gifts that the Holy Spirit has for us occur in three categories. First are the gifts of revelation. The word of wisdom is knowing how to act wisely now because of how it will affect the future. The word of knowledge is knowing something that is impossible for you to discover at the moment. Discerning of spirits is knowing what motivates people – their human spirits, demonic spirits, or the Holy Spirit. Next are the gifts of power. The gift of faith is a supernatural level of believing God to work on your behalf. The gifts of healing is supernatural authority to set people free from sicknesses, diseases, and injuries. The working of miracles, which in the original Greek language meant the "demonstration of power," is the showing forth of God's supernatural forces as the ability of God works through us. In the last category are the gifts of inspiration. The gift of prophecy is a divine ability to speak words of edification, exhortation, and comfort without having planned the message. Speaking in tongues occurs in three different manifestations. The personal use of tongues is to offer prayer or praise to God. (I Corinthians 14:2, 14-16, 28) It needs no interpretation since God understands it. Tongues can also be a sign to unbelievers.

(I Corinthians 14:22) This was the operation functioning on the Day of Pentecost when people of sixteen different languages heard the apostles speaking in their languages without having learned them. (Acts 2:8) Obviously, this usage of tongues needs no interpretation since the hearers understand automatically. The third manifestation of this gift is in giving a message for the church. (I Corinthians 14:13, 27) Unless there is a supernatural interpretation of the message, this gift is being used outside its proper scriptural order. The interpretation of tongues is the supernatural ability to translate the message given in tongues.

From the twelfth chapter of I Corinthians, we learn a lot about what these supernatural manifestations are, but we need to follow up that revelation with a thorough comprehension of the scripture in order to understand exactly how to function in these gifts properly. Our functioning in the gifts is in direct proportion to our faith. "For I say, through the grace given unto me, to every man that is among you, not to think of himself more highly than he ought to think; but to think soberly, according as God hath dealt to every man the measure of faith." (Romans 12:3) The operation of the gifts is unprofitable and useless unless we are motivated by love. "Though I speak with the tongues of men and of angels, and have not charity, I am become as sounding brass, or a tinkling cymbal. And though I have the gift of prophecy, and understand all mysteries, and all knowledge; and though I have all faith, so that I could remove mountains, and have not charity, I am nothing. And though I bestow all my goods to feed the poor, and though I give my body to be burned, and have not charity, it profiteth me nothing." (I Corinthians 13:1-3) Grace – the God-given oil of affability, courteousness, cordiality, and politeness that oils the gears so that we can live and work together – is the next necessary ingredient. "As every man hath received the gift, even so minister the same one to another, as good stewards of the manifold grace of God. If any man speak, let him speak as the oracles of God; if any man minister, let him do it as of the ability which God giveth: that God in all things may be glorified through Jesus Christ, to whom be praise and dominion for ever and ever. Amen." (I Peter 4:10-11) I remember on lady who – after being filled with the Holy Spirit – decided to prove appoint to her pastor and congregation by standing up and speaking in tongues in every service. Of course, her actions were totally out of order and the motivation behind her utterances was totally mean-spirited. Before long, she was physically hauled out of the building and forbidden to ever return. Obviously, there was no grace in her use of the spiritual gift and, therefore, nothing good was accomplished. However, when these attributes (faith, love, and grace) are in place in the life of the one who desires to operate in the gifts of the Spirit, the stage is set for a powerful manifestation of divine authority that will change the situation in which the ministry functions. Let's take a few minutes to put each of these gifts "under the microscope" and examine them a bit more in detail.

Many people feel that the supernatural gift of the word of wisdom is the same as the superior wisdom that King Solomon demonstrated when he directed that a baby be cut in two when two women claimed the same infant. (I Kings 3:16-28) Others contest that this gift has to do with foretelling the future. Actually, the matter is similar to the old Certs commercial where two individuals are arguing whether Certs is a breath mint or a candy mint. The answer was that they were both right. This gift has to do with making wise choices that will have lasting future effects as if you were able to predict the future. I once witnessed a situation in which the manager of a business felt that a certain employee had stolen a rather expensive piece of video equipment. He called in the employee and said that he had received the report that the equipment had gone missing within the past few minutes and needed him to go look for anything suspicious while the police were on their way. A few minutes later, the young man returned with the stolen item and a tale of having found them behind the building with the explanation that the thief must have stashed it there with the intent of coming back later to take it away. Everyone thought that the manager had operated in extreme wisdom to reclaim the goods while making the culprit aware that he had been caught up with even though he was allowed to save face by not being confronted directly. Unfortunately, the story doesn't end here. A few months later, this same young man was killed in the process of trying to hold up a local convenience store. Had the office manager been operating in the supernatural gift of the word of wisdom, he would have been able to see the future implications of letting the young man off without making him directly confront his wrongdoing and his dishonest heart. The young man's life and destiny were lost because someone relied on human wisdom rather than the gift of God's wisdom.

The word of knowledge is the divine operation in which God supernaturally reveals something to us that we could not possibly know in our natural human mentality. We see a number of examples of this supernatural gift in both the Old and New Testaments. Some men of God were so powerfully used in this gift that they became known as "seers." (I Samuel 9:9) Samuel was able to tell who people were and define what they were doing and thinking as soon as he met them. (I Samuel 16:4) Peter was able to know that Ananias and Sapphira had hidden money yet making a pretense that they had sacrificially given all their wealth to God. (Acts 5:3) One of the most dramatic stories of this gift in operation comes from the life of Lester Sumrall. Howard Carter had invited him to join him in ministering around the world. When Bro. Sumrall had made his arrangements to leave the States on this adventure, he had no idea where to find the older minister. He finally decided to book passage on a steamer and head to Australia with the intention of starting at the bottom of the world and working his way up until their paths crossed. The ship's first port of call on the way to Australia was a twenty-four-hour stopover in Wellington, New Zealand. During the layover, Bro. Sumrall walked the streets of the city asking people if they knew of a church "where people raised their hands and shouted *hallelujah*." When someone directed him to such a church, Sumrall went to the house next door to the church, assuming that it was the parsonage. When a gentleman came to the door, Lester started to introduce himself but was greeted with the response, "You are Lester Sumrall from America!" After recuperating from the shock of this reception, he asked how in the world the pastor would know that. The response was that Howard Carter had told the pastor to go to his home and wait for Lester's visit that afternoon and when the young man came to tell him to meet Carter in Australia in a few weeks! The gift doesn't always operate this dramatically, but it does operate with the same accuracy.

Similar to the two gifts of the Spirit that we have just looked at, the gift of discerning of spirits also has to do with supernatural revelation. In this case, it is the ability to recognize what is happening in the spiritual world. This is a very significant gift in that sometimes we don't even know what spirit is motivating ourselves. (Luke 9:55) Sometimes, we are able to discern angelic operations (Hebrews 13:2, II Kings 6:15-17); sometimes, the revelation concerns the operation of demonic spirits (Mark 8:33, Acts 5:3); and sometimes, it is the exposure of the human heart (Acts 8:23). A new employee transferred into our offices from another facility within the ministry. Since he was already an employee, there were no background checks done when he came to us. Unfortunately, it turned out that there hadn't been any checks done when he was hired at the other facility either. Apparently, he had served as a volunteer and was hired on with the assumption that all he had claimed about himself was accurate since he had proven himself to be an excellent worker in his role as a volunteer. However, there was one thing that set him apart from all the rest of us in the office – he always wanted to be addressed as "Doctor" rather than "Brother" or "Pastor" as did all the rest of us. Every time I heard him referred to with that title, I would also hear a little voice inside me say, "He's not a doctor." Eventually, I went to one of the authorities, told him about my suspicion, and suggested a background check. The result was that we discovered that he really wasn't a doctor. In fact, he had never even completed his bachelor's degree. But the more important disclosure was that he had a record as a pedophile! What's so significant about this is that he was being considered for the position as a personal counselor for the junior high boys at our Christian school! There is no way to even imagine how much damage was averted by the gift of the Spirit that allowed me to discern that spirit of deception!

The gift of faith is in operation when the Lord supernaturally drops into our hearts an above-average ability to believe for a certain thing. The story that I want to share here is so extraordinary that you may actually need a gift of faith to accept it. However, it is documented fact. When Hurricane Gloria was racing toward a landfall at Virginia Beach in 1985, an evangelist was inspired to stand on the shore of the ocean, point his finger at the approaching storm, and command it to turn out to sea. The background to this bold act of faith was that the violent winds and destructive waters imperiled the entire Christian broadcasting facility that he had labored so many years to build and that so many partners had given so sacrificially to make it a reality. Pat Robertson knew that he could not stand by and watch it all be washed away. It was at that point, that something bigger than anything he had ever known before welled up inside him and he decided to act. The weather system made an abrupt turn out to sea! Maybe there are no hurricanes threatening to ravage your life, but there are probably plenty of other storms that are wreaking havoc in your health, finances, family, and other areas of your life. If so, claim this supernatural infusion of faith to stand up, point your finger at the tempest, and make it back off. Join the great men and women who exercised this gift and turned the tables of their destinies.

> Who through faith subdued kingdoms, wrought righteousness, obtained promises, stopped the mouths of lions, Quenched the violence of fire, escaped the edge of the sword, out of weakness were made strong, waxed valiant in fight, turned to flight the armies of the aliens. Women received their dead raised to life again: and others were tortured, not accepting deliverance; that they might obtain a better resurrection. (Hebrews 11:33-35)

The gift of working miracles is similar to the gift of faith except that this gift has to do with what God does through you rather than for you. In the story that we just related about Hurricane Gloria, Pat Robertson didn't do anything more than point his finger at the storm. On the other hand, the gift of miracles involves some physical involvement on the part of the recipient. We can trace this pattern throughout the scripture. When Moses wanted to draw water out of a rock, he had to strike the boulder with his staff. (Exodus 17:6) When Elijah wanted to supernaturally provide for a widow and her son, he demanded that she take the action of making a cake for him. (I Kings 17:13) When Elisha wanted to create a supernatural income stream for a widow whose boys were to be taken from the home to work as servants to pay off a debt, he told her that she had to collect a quantity of pots. (II Kings 4:3-4) When Jesus wanted to make supernatural wine, He had the servants fill huge pots with water. (John 2:7) I could relate one Bible story after another to illustrate this truth; however, I'm sure that you see the pattern by now, but let's bring the message into our contemporary situation. If you want to see people healed supernaturally, you will have to lay hands on them. If you want to see your finances supernaturally increased, you will have to learn how to trust God more boldly by giving sacrificially in faith. If you want to see people who are tormented by demons set free, you'll have to muster the courage to boldly confront them. In other words, miracles happen when we act! When one of my students was ministering on the mission field, a pastor asked him to go pray for a man who was beleaguered by so many demons that he was kept in a cage to protect both himself and everyone nearby. My student said that he knew in his heart that the only way the man would be free was that he would be bold enough to go inside the cage with him. Putting the key in the padlock was the action necessary to trigger the miracle. Once you find the right key, you'll see miracles, too!

Healing is the only gift that is listed as being plural in nature – the gifts of healing. This is because the same gift exhibits itself in many different manifestations. All the manifestations of the gift result in the healing of a sickness, disease, injury, or disability; however, different individuals seem to have certain ailments that they see healed more frequently. Some people tend to see more results when they minister to people with deaf ears, while others seem to see more blind eyes opened. For others, it might be cancers or tumors. The final class in my course on the gifts of the Spirit was planned as a day of impartation and manifestation. I had asked the students to spend some time in prayer and fasting, seeking the Lord about what gift or gifts they should be operating in. (I Corinthians 12:31, 14:1) In that final session, I gave each student the opportunity to activate the gift that he felt God was leading him to operate in. When one young man said that he felt that he was to operate in the gifts of healing, I asked if there were anyone in the class who needed a healing. Eventually, one student acknowledged that she had sustained a serious back injury several months before. She then added, however, that she knew that a certain evangelist who had the gift of healing for back injuries would be in town in the next few months and she was waiting for his visit to be healed. At that point, I asked if she really wanted to suffer for several months while waiting for the renowned healer or receive her healing that day at the hands of her classmate. Reluctantly, she submitted to having prayer that day and was instantly healed! The moral of that little story is that healing – and all the other gifts – is a gift of God. Therefore, it doesn't matter whom He chooses to use to deliver his gift. Think of it this way. If you order an item from a shopping website, it makes no difference if they send it by Fed Ex, UPS, the postal service, or drop it on your front porch from a drone. All that matters is that you get the merchandise!

I often have people challenge me concerning the next gift – speaking in tongues – with arguments that it doesn't do anything useful. They say that the Bible says that it is better to prophesy because it blesses other people whereas speaking in tongues doesn't help others. Of course, their point is well founded in I Corinthians chapter fourteen.

> He that speaketh in an unknown tongue edifieth himself; but he that prophesieth edifieth the church. (I Corinthians 14:4)

*For thou verily givest thanks well, but the
other is not edified. (I Corinthians 14:17)*

However, it is pertinent that we understand that in this chapter Paul was correcting the excessive use of tongues in public meetings. Indeed, he went so far in verse twenty-three to say that the way they were operating in the gift actually made them look like crazy people. But the thing that we have to realize here is that Paul never minimized the gift itself, only the way that the members of the church in Corinth were implementing it. In fact, Paul validated the gift by saying that it was a vital part of his own life. (I Corinthians 14:18) So what is the bottom line on this issue? Speaking in tongues may not encourage and strengthen the congregation like prophesying does; however, it does strengthen the individual believer in his personal faith. (I Corinthians 14:4, Romans 8:26-28, Jude 20) And it takes strong Christians to be able to bless and encourage others. Therefore, speaking in tongues does bless the church – howbeit, indirectly.

Over the years, I've heard the issue debated many times why God instituted the gift of speaking in tongues. One of the standard answers is that tongues is a secret code language between man and God that allows them to communicate without the devil's being able to decode their private messages. I have never accepted that argument on a couple points. First, such an explanation would undermine the power of prayer in the known language. If the fact that Satan can understand what you are saying gives him some sort of advantage, then praying in our understanding is detrimental. However, we are repeatedly commanded to pray using our normal vocabulary. (I Corinthians 14:15) Additionally, just because the devil understands what is being said doesn't necessarily give him an advantage. He could read every prophecy in the Old Testament predicting the coming of Christ and His redemptive death; however, just because He could read the words did not mean that he could understood the message. First Corinthians 2:8 explains that had he understood what he was doing, he would never have inspired men to crucify Jesus. He instituted his own undoing by not being able to interpret Isaiah chapter fifty-three and Psalm twenty-two. In the book of Daniel, we find a very good example of how the devil – and his men – can read something and totally miss the message. When the Lord wrote a message to Babylon and their king on the palace wall, Belshazzar called for all the astrologers, Chaldeans, soothsayers, and wise men of his empire to try to interpret the message. Every one of the men could read the words – which all happened to be the names of coins that they all were carrying about in their purses. They had no idea why God Himself would bother with sending them a personally handwritten message about pocket change. It was only Daniel who recognized that each of the words had a second meaning – much like our term "nickel" refers to a five-cent coin but is also the name of a kind of metal. When Daniel read the message using the other meanings for the words, it spelled the doom of the nation. (Daniel 5:5-28)

The second reason that I have rejected this explanation is that I'm not convinced that Satan cannot understand tongues. I Corinthians 13:1 explains that tongues are the languages of men and angels. Satan was originally an angel; therefore, he spoke the language of angels. I really doubt that he forgot his original tongue just because he was cast out of heaven. He also understands every language of men; otherwise, how would he be able to tempt them and put wrong thoughts into their minds? A couple chapters ago, I told you that I was going to share an amazing experience about the supernatural gift of tongues – and it is coming up in the next paragraph – but allow me to jump ahead a bit and say that it will have to do with the Hindi language. That being said, I wish to remind you that nine hundred million people pray to the devil in Hindi each day; so, he certainly understands that language. If he understands their prayers, he can obviously understand the language if it is one that God chooses to give someone when he is speaking in tongues. I believe that the real reason God instituted the gift of tongues is that it requires men to trust Him in a totally new and radical way. When we speak in tongues, we are no longer in control of the words that are coming out of our mouths — a totally new foreign experience. If we can't trust God that what we are saying is really of Him, we fail the faith test.

When we come to the next gift that Paul listed in I Corinthians chapter twelve – the gift of interpreting tongues – we have to see it in conjunction with the gift of tongues since they go together, as Frank Sinatra would say, like love and marriage and a horse and carriage. There are conditions when the gift of tongues can operate independently – when it is a prayer language for a believer and when it is a miraculous sign to an unbeliever – but in the church, this gift should always function in tandem with the gift of interpretation. (I Corinthians 14:13, 27-28) When these two gifts are in operation, one person will supernaturally speak in a language that he or she has never learned. This miraculous utterance will be followed by someone else who will speak out the same message that was just given in an unknown language but this time it will be in the language that everyone understands. The operation of these two gifts in conjunction is a supernatural demonstration to prove the validity of the message – as we will see in the following example. One Sunday morning, I was at the pulpit of our church ready to receive the tithes and offerings when a lady stood up and gave a message in tongues. I asked the Holy Spirit to give me the interpretation and then spoke out the words that I felt He had inspired me to say. Once the message was given, we went on with the service. The next morning, one of my students came to me before class to discuss the event. When I told him that it was simply the operation of these two supernatural gifts of the Holy Spirit, he responded by saying that he felt that I didn't really understand what had happened. When I asked why he would say such a thing, he said, "Well, I'm from India and my native language is Hindi. When the woman spoke, she was speaking in perfect Hindi. Then when you spoke, you gave an exact word-for-word translation of everything that she said." Of course, the woman had no way of knowing even one word of Hindi – much less enough to give a full exhortation. Even though I have been to India more times that I can remember, I didn't even know enough of the language to recognize that the lady was speaking Hindi.

Many people think of the gift of prophecy as the ability to predict the future; however, others argue that it is not forecasting coming events since Paul defined this operation as edification, exhortation, and comfort. (I Corinthians 14:3) Again, I'd like to employ the Certs commercial in trying to answer this matter. Just because prophecy speaks to the at-hand needs of a person does not preclude that it can also speak into the future. For example: if a brother who has an issue with low self-esteem, he needs to be encouraged and built up – "edified" in biblical language. If the Holy Spirit gives someone an encouraging word to remedy the gentleman's self-esteem issue, that is the gift of prophecy in operation. Suppose that word contains a statement like, "God is going to use you to bless others." In that case, there is an element of futuristic prediction involved as well as present-day encouragement. For a second example: if a sister is just about to "throw in the towel," she needs to be challenged to continue to "hang in there" – "exhortation" in King James terminology. If the Holy Spirit gives someone an inspiring word to get her "over the hump," that is the gift of prophecy in operation. Suppose that word contains a statement like, "You are going to make it; you are not going to fail!" In that case, there is an element of futuristic prognosis involved as well as present-day inspiration. For a third example: if a couple have lost a baby, they need consolation – "comfort" in this passage. If the Holy Spirit gives someone a reassuring word to relieve their sorrows, that is the gift of prophecy in operation. Suppose that word contains a statement like, "You are going to see that baby again in heaven." In that case, there is an element of futuristic expectation involved as well as present-day consolation. Therefore, the gift of prophecy is the ability to speak into people's lives under the Holy Spirit's anointing and direction in a way to help today and into the future.

The Holy Spirit – A Gift that Must Not Be Hindered

A friend of mine had become very interested in the baptism in the Holy Spirit. During the weeks following, we had Bible study sessions together, and I tried to help her understand what the Holy Spirit baptism is and how to receive it. I was shocked – to say the least – when she came to me one day and said that she had decided to have nothing else to do with this subject "because tongues divide churches." What was the problem? Somewhere she had encountered what might be called the "blabtism." This experience had driven her away from the real baptism.

The dictionary defines "blab" as:
1) to reveal indiscreetly and thoughtlessly
2) to talk or chatter indiscreetly and thoughtlessly
3) idle, indiscreet chattering
4) a person who blabs

These definitions sound very much like the biblical description of speaking in tongues when not motivated by love and wisdom:
1) a sounding brass or a tinkling cymbal (I Corinthians 13:1)
2) making noise (I Corinthians 14:7-8)
3) speaking to the air. (I Corinthians 14:9)

The point here is not that we should stop speaking in tongues or that we should try to stop others from speaking (I Corinthians 14:39) since the Bible clearly states that it would be good if each Christian were a tongues speaker (I Corinthians 14:39); rather, the point is that the gifts must be ministered in love. Love does not behave itself unseemly (I Corinthians 13:5) and never fails (I Corinthians 13:8). However, without the ingredient of love, the gifts are likely to behave themselves unseemly and to fail. (I Corinthian 13:1) Without the ingredient of wisdom, they are likely to make others think that Spirit-filled people are crazy. (I Corinthians 14:23)

We must be very careful to avoid the obstacles that can become roadblocks that hinder us and others from receiving this all-important gift from the Lord. I have learned from many experiences that God is very eager for believers to receive the power of the Holy Spirit. He knows how important these gifts are and wants His children to have them. One young man, after talking with me, was so concerned that I was in error over this Holy Ghost doctrine that he went home to pray for me. Down on his knees, he began to intercede that I would find the truth and be released from error. The major problem he encountered was that he could not say the word "error" because his own language had been changed to unknown tongues by that point. Another friend of mine received the baptism in the Holy Spirit while driving down a steep and winding mountain road. He was so overjoyed with his experience that he threw his hands into the air and began to praise God in his new language. Only God could have gotten his car safely down that twisty mountain road! One of my favorite stories on this topic has to do with one of my close college friends who had been raised in a Pentecostal church and was very desirous to receive this spiritual baptism. In fact, it had been thirteen years that he had been praying for this blessing. One afternoon, a fellow student whom he was trying to lead to salvation confronted him with the question, "How do you know that it will really work?" His answer was, "You have to accept it by faith." Just then, the Holy Spirit spoke to his heart, "Yes, and that's how you have to receive my baptism – by faith." The "better idea light bulb" suddenly flashed on inside his spirit, and he understood why he had been hindered for so many years. That evening, he released his faith and was inundated by the most spectacular flood of the Holy Spirit

I have ever witnessed. For the next two days, he could not talk on the phone, answer a question in class, or order a meal in the campus cafeteria. He literally found it impossible to force himself to speak English. I guess it was all the praise that had been pent up inside him for more than a dozen years that suddenly came rushing out!

As we have already observed, the most important thing to remember about receiving the fullness of the Holy Spirit is that Jesus said that it was as simple as asking our earthly fathers for the things that they naturally want to provide for their children. (Luke 11:11-13) In other words, we don't have to beg or plead; we just expect that God is instantly ready to give us this great promise. Again, as we have already noticed, Paul called this confidence in asking, "faith." (Galatians 3:2) In essence, we don't work to earn the gift; we simply expect that God wants to give it to us. We don't have to be good enough; we simply have to be His children.

I have encountered many people who have had difficulty understanding this truth. Some have told me of their failures during their Christian life and concluded with the evaluation that they don't deserve the gift since their lives have been less than perfect. My response is always that they deserve it more than those who haven't had such failures because one of the works of the Holy Spirit is to sanctify us. (II Thessalonians 2:13, I Peter 1:2) Others have told me that they have waited for the perfect time when God was ready to give them the gift. My response to that is to point them to the passage we have already referred to in which Jesus compared our receiving the Holy Spirit to a father giving his son a piece of bread or a fish. I then say that if they are spiritually hungry, God is as ready to give them the Holy Spirit as an earthly father is to feed his physically hungry children. When one young Filipino man told me that he was waiting for God's timing, I responded that God's timing was in AD 33 and that meant that he was almost two thousand years late in receiving. At that, he instantly burst into tears and a beautiful prayer language began to flow out of him!

In my ministry all over the world, I have encountered many individuals who have had similar blockages in receiving the manifestation of the infilling of the Holy Spirit, and I observed that – almost without exception – they are struggling with one or more of these five problems:

1) They are afraid that they might have a counterfeit. However, Luke 11:13 tells us that it is God who gives us the Holy Spirit. "If ye then, being evil, know how to give good gifts unto your children: how much more shall your heavenly Father give the Holy Spirit to them that ask him?"

2) They are concerned that the words they speak might be something that they made up themselves. However, Acts 2:4 tells us that the words (utterance) come from the Holy Spirit. "And they were all filled with the Holy Ghost, and began to speak...as the Spirit gave them utterance."

3) They think that Holy Spirit is going to physically take over their mouths and make them speak in tongues. However, we can turn to Acts 2:4 again to see that we have to cooperate with the Holy Spirit by actually speaking by moving our lips and giving voice to the words that are in our hearts. "And they were all filled with the Holy Ghost, and began to speak with other tongues..."

4) They think that they have to be good enough or somehow earn the gift. However, Galatians 3:2 confirms that we receive the Holy Spirit by faith alone, not good works. "This only would I learn

of you, Received ye the Spirit by the works of the law, or by the hearing of faith?"

5) They think that the language will come out of their minds like speaking in our normal language does. However, John 7:38-39 records the words of Jesus in which He explained that they would come out of our belly (the spirit man) rather than out of our mind. "He that believeth on me, as the scripture hath said, out of his belly shall flow rivers of living water. (But this spake he of the Spirit, which they that believe on him should receive: for the Holy Ghost was not yet given; because that Jesus was not yet glorified.)" A recent study done by the University of Pennsylvania found that frontal lobe activity which is associated with language and willful control of the body decreases during speaking in tongues. In other words, there really is a force other than the speaker who is motivating the speaking. Another interesting discovery in this study was the difference between the experience of glossolalia (speaking in tongues) and Buddhist and Catholic meditation; these other activities actually increased the frontal lobe brain activity, indicating the participants' active involvement.

I have observed that even some who have desired, asked in faith, and had hands laid on them have failed to receive any manifestation of the infilling of the Holy Spirit. I believe that this is because they failed at the very last step – activation. As Paul told his spiritual son in II Timothy 1:6, we need to stir up the gift that came inside of us when we were prayed over by the church leaders. I believe that stirring up that gift can come at the initial infilling of the Spirit by allowing the Holy Spirit to give you a new language. Many people insist upon continuing to speak in their native language and expect the Holy Spirit to override their words. Others refuse to say anything and just wait for the Holy Spirit to make them begin to speak in tongues. On the Day of Pentecost, the apostles set the pattern when they did the speaking as the Holy Spirit gave them utterance.

In Luke 11:11-13, we find the very words of Jesus Himself, telling us that the gift of the Holy Spirit (including speaking with tongues) is a present that the Heavenly Father will willingly give to His children. In Mark 16:17, Jesus added that this gift was readily available to all who would believe. Notice that the promise wasn't to pastors, elders, saints, or people in any specific time period; it was for all who would believe. In fact, Peter clarified the promise in Acts 2:39 by saying that it was for the people present, their children, and to all that are afar off – even as many as the Lord our God shall call. As we have already noted as we took our little tour through the book of Acts, there is a definite connection between receiving the infilling of the Holy Spirit and the supernatural manifestation of the gift of speaking in tongues. So why shouldn't all the believers in Acts chapter twenty-nine (those of us who continue the story after the close of the New Testament) also receive this blessing?

The Holy Spirit - Our Life Transformer

Likewise the Spirit also helpeth our infirmities: for we know not what we should pray for as we ought: but the Spirit itself maketh intercession for us with groanings which cannot be uttered. And he that searcheth the hearts knoweth what is the mind of the Spirit, because he maketh intercession for the saints according to the will of God. And we know that all things work together for good to them that love God, to them who are the called according to his purpose. (Romans 8:26-28)

In the book of Romans, Paul made it explicitly clear that the Holy Spirit must take an active role in our prayers if we want them to be successful. Because the Holy Spirit knows the mind of God, He can help our prayers by assuring that they are in the perfect will of God. At that point, we can know unquestionably that all things are going to work out for our best! What a promise!

The real power of prayer is the guidance of the Holy Spirit and the real substance of prayer is God's Word. Unfortunately, we all too often pray prayers that originate in our own imagination and desires. Such prayers may not be related at all to the will of God concerning the matter. On the other hand, we know that the Holy Spirit is always in tune with the will of God and that the Word of God is the perfect expression of His will; therefore, if we are able to unite these two unquestionable articulations of the will of God as we pray, we can't go wrong. In my personal life, I have found that I can combine this truth with a principle from Paul's discussion on the armor of God – that praying in the Spirit is brandishing the sword of the Spirit (the Word of God) – to develop a surefire prayer model. (Ephesians 6:17-18) I begin by praying in tongues until the Holy Spirit quickens my spirit with an individual or situation that I should pray for that day. Invariably, He will also prompt me with a specific scripture that relates to that specific need. I then spend a few minutes proclaiming that scriptural promise or principle over the person or issue. Once I feel a peace about the prayer, I return to praying in tongues until I am prompted to pray for another individual of situation.

While we are considering the Holy Spirit's association with the armor of God, let's take a quick look at a passage that – although it does not specifically mention speaking in tongues or the Holy Spirit – reveals some powerful truth about the weapons of spiritual warfare. It seems totally obvious that the renewing of our minds that gives us victory over the destructive forces of the enemy would certainly be the work of the Holy Spirit – and likely through the process of speaking in tongues.

> *The weapons of our warfare are not carnal, but mighty through God to the pulling down of strong holds; Casting down imaginations...and bringing into captivity every thought to the obedience of Christ. (II Corinthians 10:4-5)*

In this passage the Apostle Paul taught us that we have weapons that are mighty through God that enable us to subdue our carnal minds. Certainly, there are many aspects to the spiritual forces that we can use in this conquest of our rebellious thoughts; however, speaking in tongues is almost unquestionably one of them. After all, Paul's definition of these weapons is that they are not carnal, or related to anything that could be mustered up by our natural abilities – a perfect definition of the supernatural gift of speaking in a language that we have not learned through our own human intellectual abilities. Paul further explained that these weapons result in the dislodging of our erroneous human way of thinking and they establish our thoughts under the authority of Christ. In I Corinthians 14:14, he explained that praying in tongues is prayer from our spiritual man that supersedes anything that goes on in our human intellect. It does exactly what we expect of the mighty weapons of God – it brings the spiritual man into dominance and the carnal man into a submissive state. No matter how determined we may be, we can never renew our minds through our own efforts; yet, as we practice this spiritual exercise, we'll find that it becomes easier and easier to have a Christ-like mentality.

Jesus called the Holy Spirit the Spirit of truth. (John 14:17, 15:26, 16:13) He went on to add that the Holy Spirit would speak to us all that He learned from Jesus and that the result would be that He would be able to reveal things that are to come. Jesus is the truth (John 14:6; Revelation 3:7, 14; 19:9, 11; 21:5; 22:6), but it is the Holy Spirit who reveals Him to us. Paul made a special point of praying for the believers at Ephesus that they would have the advantage of the revelatory power of the Holy Spirit because he knew that it is only through the Holy Spirit's enlightenment that they would ever know the power residing in them through Christ. "[I] cease not to give thanks for you, making mention of you in my prayers; That the God of our Lord Jesus Christ, the Father of glory, may give unto you the spirit of wisdom and revelation in the knowledge of him: The eyes of your understanding being enlightened; that ye may know what is the hope of his calling, and what the riches of the glory of his inheritance in the saints, And what is the exceeding greatness of his power to us-ward who believe, according to the working of his mighty power." (Ephesians 1:16-19) Writing to the Corinthians, he quoted the prophet Isaiah, "Eye hath not seen, nor ear heard, neither have entered into the heart of man, the things which God hath prepared for them that love him." (I Corinthians 2:9, Isaiah 64:4) But he then immediately added, "But God hath revealed them unto us by his Spirit: for the Spirit searcheth all things, yea, the deep things of God." (verse 10) Even the great prophet Isaiah didn't have a clue as to all the victories we can experience when we are led by the Holy Spirit's wisdom and revelation – the truth of Christ. Additionally, John 16:13 states, "When he, the Spirit of truth, is come, he will guide you into all truth." There are so many deceptions in the world that can destroy us, but we have this powerful promise from Jesus that there is a source of truth that we can tap into and find security and safety.

Jesus told us that the Holy Spirit would glorify the Lord. (John 16:14) In a world that seems intent on dishonoring God, we really need this aspect of the work of the Holy Spirit. With Darwinism dominating our educational system, telling us repeatedly that random chance is to be credited for our incredibly complex and beautiful world, we need the Holy Spirit to prompt us to acknowledge His handiwork. (Psalm 102:25) With abortionists constantly shouting at us that human life is no more than mass of tissue and is in no way a representation of the likeness of God, we need the Holy Spirit to remind us that the heavenly Father has fearfully and wondrously shaped us in His very image. (Genesis 1:27, Psalm 139:14) With the gay agenda constantly in our faces insisting that every form of perversion is acceptable, we need the Holy Spirit to glorify the Lord by giving us a pattern of the righteousness and holiness of the Father and the purity of the Son. (Psalm 29:2)

Another aspect of the work of the Holy Spirit is that He testifies of Jesus. (John 15:26) Again, we live in a desperate world that needs constant reminders of the life and love of Jesus. Not only does the unregenerate world need the Holy Spirit's message, we believers need to be constantly made aware that Jesus has set a standard of holiness for us through His sinless life (Hebrews 4:15), but at the same time has made a way for us to be forgiven when we fail to measure up on that yardstick (Romans 3:23, I John 1:8). We, as well as the fallen world around us, need to be continually made mindful of the tremendous sacrifice that Jesus paid to demonstrate His love for us and of the amazing authority that He passed on to us through His unparalleled victory over death and the devil. Additionally, the Holy Spirit speaks about us as definitively as He does about the Godhead. The Apostle Paul declared that we have received the Spirit of adoption, whereby we cry, "Abba, Father." (Romans 8:15) In the fallen world we live in, it is vitally important that we also have a voice that is calling out something about us as well as about God Himself. It is the work of the Holy Spirit to confirm inside each of us that God is not a distant reality, separate from us and our daily situation. No, we are His very children, and He cares for us!

Allow me to introduce the next biblical concept with a short anecdote. The little boy excitedly ripped open his package of animal crackers and very carefully began to lay them all out on the kitchen table. Suddenly, he began to cry and ran away from the table. His mother chased after him and drew his tearstained face close to her apron, asking what was the matter. Between the sobs, he blurted out that he had read the warning on the box, "Do not eat if the seal is broken." Yes, it's just a humorous little story, but the truth is that many of us are just as clueless as this little boy when it comes to understanding what the seal of the Spirit really is. You see, the seal of the Spirit has to do with our protection, not salvation. According to Ephesians 1:13, we are "sealed with that holy Spirit of promise." The Holy Spirit has put a seal, a guarantee, on us that means that we cannot be tampered with. We are tamperproof and the devil doesn't have any right to get a hold on us. Knowing this enables us to live our lives in continual victory. The seal of God on our lives marks us, distinguishes us, and preserves us. In biblical times when a letter or a package was shipped from one place to another, wax was put across the envelope or the package and a seal or signet ring was stamped into that hot wax to leave a distinct and unique identification. The seal served two purposes. It made sure that no one tampered with the package so that when it was received it would be in exactly the same condition as when it was sent. When the envelope still had the wax on it with the seal in place, everyone knew that no one else had opened it. Another thing a seal did was to identify who it was that put the package together. Each seal was characteristic of the individual sender. No two individuals had identical seals. It is impossible to counterfeit the unique seal that God has placed on each believer. Our seal is the Holy Ghost.

In 1982, seven individuals in the Chicago area died of potassium cyanide poisoning from Extra-Strength Tylenol capsules that had been tampered with after the medicine was delivered to the pharmacies in the area. These poisonings led to reforms in the packaging of over-the-counter substances and to federal anti-tampering laws. In 2003, a batch of worm-infested candy in India prompted the Cadbury Company to implement a new double-sealed wrapper for the customers' protection. Just like these products in the grocery stores and pharmacies are marked, "Do not purchase if the seal has been broken," we must ensure that the seal on our lives has not been broken. We can do this by always submitting to the conviction of the Holy Spirit when He reproves sin and error in our lives. (John 16:8) Each time we do a wrong thing, think a wrong thought, or have a wrong attitude, the Holy Spirit causes an uneasiness in our spirit man. Our proper response must be to immediately acknowledge His warning and repent of that error. If we refuse to yield to His wooing, we damage that seal and, therefore, jeopardize our purity by allowing contaminants into our hearts. Paul frequently mentioned his good or pure conscience. (Acts 23:1, Romans 9:1, II Corinthians 1:12, I Timothy 1:5, II Timothy 1:3) He knew the power of living his life free from tampering with the seal that the Holy Spirit placed upon his heart. I can imagine that he must have learned a lesson from the story of David's defeat of Goliath. The stone from the shepherd's sling found that singular point of vulnerability in the giant's armor – the opening between his eyes. (I Samuel 17:49) Paul realized that the enemy could and would take advantage of even the slightest glitch in his armor in just the same way that David had taken advantage of the almost unnoticeable breach in the giant's protection. Therefore, he constantly made sure that he kept his tamperproof seal intact through carefully guarding his conscience. Many preachers teach that we cannot trust our consciences – probably because they do not understand the difference between our natural conscience that can be corrupted and nullified and the Holy Spirit directed conscience that is always as accurate as God Himself. By simply looking into the scriptures, we can see how important it is to follow this renewed conscience.

> I say the truth in Christ, I lie not, my conscience also bearing me witness in the Holy Ghost. (Romans 9:1)

> Now the end of the commandment is charity out of a pure heart, and of a good conscience, and of faith unfeigned. (I Timothy 1:5)

One of the first advantages that Jesus pointed out to His disciples concerning the work of the Holy Spirit was that He would reprove the world of sin, righteousness, and judgment. (John 16:8)   Although some Bible teachers conclude that this verse does not apply to Christians since it speaks of the "world," the Greek word used here is a generic term for the created order or all the humans within it. The term is also widely used to refer to the totality of the human population – which would include believers as well as unbelievers. The word, "reprove" is actually a legal term referring to the cross examination of a witness in the court of law. If you've ever been present for a trial – or even watched a movie or television show depicting a trial – you can relate to the unique power of a skillful cross-examination. Once the attorney for the prosecution "grills" the witness with questions that elicit answers that imply the defendant's guilt, the attorney for the defense will question the same witness about the same events; however, this time the questions will be asked from a carefully strategized angle to evoke answers that suggest the defendant's innocence. One minute, we assume that the individual is guilty; the next minute, we are convinced that he is not. Why? Because of the cross-examination. The same thing happens when the Holy Spirit shows up in our lives. He asks questions from a totally new angle that makes us totally rethink our lives. What we've been able to excuse before suddenly becomes inexcusable. What we've previously seen as insurmountable now becomes manageable. What was a mountain before is miraculously transformed into a molehill and vice versa. That's why it is expedient that we receive and welcome the Holy Spirit's cross-examination of our lives and attitudes. This cross-examining comes in the form of a Holy Spirit directed conscience that is as radically different from our natural conscience as is the defense attorney's examination from the prosecution's attorney.

Allow me to illustrate what I mean by that statement with a story from the life of Dr. Lester Sumrall. When Dr. Sumrall was ministering in the remote jungles of South

America, he preached to tribes of indigenous people who were so far separated from modern civilization that they had never seen a white man before. As he ministered to these primitive people, many of them opened their hearts to Jesus and prayed with Bro. Sumrall to become Christians. Then, a very unusual thing happened. The women came to him after the closing prayer and asked if he happened to have an extra piece of cloth in his backpack. Before he answered them, he asked why they were interested. Their reply was that after they had prayed with him they somehow felt that they should cover their breasts. Then Dr. Sumrall reminded them that no other women in the tribe were wearing anything above the waist and questioned why they felt that they wanted to do something that was different from everyone else. Their reply was that they didn't understand but that they just felt that it was the right thing to do. What an outstanding example of how the Holy Spirit had reproved – cross-examined – these women without any human influence or involvement!

In Ephesians 4:30, we learn that God has sealed us unto the day of redemption, meaning that He has put an identifying mark on our lives that unquestionably indicates that we are uniquely preserved for a new perfect world until the day that we are delivered from this present corrupted world. Perhaps it is in Romans 15:16 that we get a glimpse into what that identifying mark is. Here the Apostle says that the Holy Ghost has sanctified us – an expression that speaks of being exclusively set apart for God and His purposes. It is the work of the Holy Spirit to prompt us toward activities, attitudes, and thoughts that fulfill the nature and purposes of God and to protect us from activities, attitudes, and thoughts that go against His nature and purposes. In Romans 8:14 and Galatians 5:16 we learn more about how this whole process works. It is by the leading of the Spirit. As we are led by the promptings of the Holy Spirit, our sonship in the heavenly family is established and our victory over the worldly influences that are contrary to that sonship is manifest.

Ephesians 4:30 also introduces the idea of grieving the Holy Spirit. It would be a lopsided argument to stress the Holy Spirit's role in sealing us and ignore the possibility of our grieving Him. It seems to me that we can understand this principal a bit more clearly by considering the breastplate of righteous that Paul described as part of the armor of God in Ephesians chapter six. Given the context of the Ephesian passage, I'm certain that the apostle was thinking more of the Roman soldier's breastplate that would be worn by a soldier to protect his vital organs during battle than the Jewish high priest's breastplate that was worn by the high priest of Israel as a means of receiving direction from God. However, I'd like to beg your indulgence for a few minutes to consider the suggestion that there are some significant messages to be gained if we also imagine the possibility that the Old Testament breastplate could also be playing into his thinking. Called the breastplate of judgment, this garment that bore the names of the tribes of Israel and contained the Urim and the Thummim – which were used to receive definitive messages from God – was to be worn close to the heart when the high priest went before the Lord. (Exodus 28:29)

The first relationship that I'd like to draw between the priest's breastplate and the breastplate of righteousness would be that the priest's garment had stones representing each of the tribes of Israel embroidered into the breastplate. In similar fashion, a warrior's breastplate would often have the seal or crest of his country fashioned into the metal. In both cases, the breastplate served as a form of identification. Spiritually, our righteousness is a product of our identity with Christ. (Romans 3:22, 5:21; I Corinthians 1:30; Philippians 1:11,

3:9; II Peter 1:1) If we do not know Christ, we will never be righteous, but in knowing Him, a righteousness that supersedes all our efforts is established through faith in Jehovah Tsidkenu – the God Who is Our Righteousness! Since the seal, or signet, of biblical times was the identifying mark similar to branding cattle in more contemporary history, it is easy to see how there could be a parallel with the priest's breastplate that bore the stones of the tribes of Israel and the soldier's breastplate that bore the symbol of Rome. However, the parallel doesn't stop there. The priest's breastplate contained a pocket in which the Urim and the Thummim were kept. These stones were a way in which the Lord revealed His will and judgment to the people of Israel. Perhaps there is even a parallel between these oracle stones and the qualities of faith and love that Paul identified with our breastplate in I Thessalonians 5:8; without faith and love, we will never manifest God's will in our lives. In the same way, the Holy Spirit not only identifies us as the people of God but also speaks the will of God for our lives and identifies when we are in accordance with that will and when we are not. (John 16:8) The Holy Spirit's job is to reprove of sin (when we are out of the will of God), of righteousness (when we are in the will of God), and of judgment (the consequences of being either in or out of the will of God). As the Holy Spirit continually draws our attention to what is right and wrong, He preserves our hearts just like a soldier's breastplate protects his vital organs; therefore, he leads us into all righteousness. (Romans 8:4, Galatians 5:16) One last association that I'd like to consider is the closeness to the heart that was mentioned in Exodus 28:29 when describing the priest's breastplate. Since the breastplate of a soldier was always worn over the chest to protect the vital organs, especially the heart, it would seem logical that Paul chose the breastplate as his symbol when he wanted to talk about righteousness because the heart has to be associated with righteousness. (Deuteronomy 9:5; I Kings 3:6; Nehemiah 9:8; Job 27:6; Psalm 15:2, 32:11, 36:10, 40:10, 64:10, 94:15, 97:11, 119:7; Proverbs 15:28; Isaiah 51:7; Jeremiah 20:12; Ezekiel 13:22; Romans 10:10; II Timothy 2:22)

In terms of relating the seal of the Spirit to the breastplate of righteousness, let me ask you just one simple question, "Where do you feel it every time you do something wrong or something good?" The obvious answer is, "In the heart." It is a biblical principle that the emotions of our hearts are activated by our right and wrong actions. (Psalm 32:11, 64:10, 69:20, 73:21; Acts 2:37) Solomon warned us to keep our hearts with all diligence because the issues of life flow out of them. (Proverbs 4:23) In the New Testament we see how God has made it easy for us. If we don't grieve the Holy Spirit by disregarding His promptings, He will become a breastplate of righteous actions and thoughts to guard our hearts. When the Apostle Paul warned us against grieving the Holy Spirit, he used a Greek term that takes us far beyond what most of us have ever considered. His wording here speaks of a deep emotional wound like that which is inflicted when jilted by a lover. First of all, many of us never stop to think that the Holy Spirit is a personality with all the same qualities that we humans share. He has emotions and can be insulted and offended by our actions just as another human can. When we disregard an impression He has placed in our hearts, it is not just a nebulous, impersonal impulse that we are dealing with – it is a living, emotional personality that has been rejected. Even when we do realize that our ignoring or contradicting the wooing and prompting of the Holy Spirit is a personal offense against a living personality, we generally fail to understand the intensity of our actions. Just think how deep the wound and how long the healing process associated with the breakup of lovers or a divorce. Now take that to the infinite level on which God lives. This is the picture Paul was trying to paint for us to understand how significant our response to the Holy Spirit can be. Notice that he also intensifies the passage by adding that the Holy Spirit's work is to seal us unto the day of redemption. The message that Paul is trying to communicate here is that our responses to the Holy Spirit's directions are not just for the moment, but they have eternal consequences, effecting our eternal destinies.

The Holy Spirit – Our Life Coach

In John 16:7, Jesus said that it was expedient for us that He should go away because unless He left, the Holy Spirit could not come. What is this advantage that Jesus spoke of concerning having the Holy Spirit in our lives?

The book of Romans is actually the closest thing to a systematic theology that we have in the New Testament. Because Paul wrote it to a church that he had never visited and to a congregation of folks whom he did not know, he was not able to address very specific issues. Instead, he gave them a thorough explanation of the gospel in general. The progression of the book is that chapters one through five set the theological stage for salvation, chapter six gives the salvation experience, chapter seven describes post-salvation existence lived in human power, chapter eight gives his victorious answer through the Spirit, and chapters nine through sixteen give practical application of Christian life. Paul's emphasis in chapter seven is on the word "I" – his personal effort to achieve godly goals. The conclusion is that it is impossible to do so. He ends chapter seven in defeat, but moves into chapter eight with great victory. The key to this dramatic shift is that in chapter eight he moved into the realm of walking in the Spirit. Paul speaks of the Spirit only four times in the first seven chapters of Romans, but twenty times in chapter eight alone. Since the original Greek texts contain no capital letters, the translators have made their own evaluations as to when to use "Spirit" (as Holy Spirit) and when to write "spirit" (as in human spirit); therefore, it is sometimes difficult to clearly distinguish whether Paul actually meant the Holy Spirit or the human spirit in some of the verses. However, I like to think of how a tuning fork will automatically begin to vibrate in resonance when another tuning fork of the same pitch is sounded. If our human spirit is on the same "wave length" with the Holy

Spirit, they will both be "singing the same song" so it doesn't really matter if the text is actually talking about the divine or the human spirit – they are both functioning alike.

If we determine to walk according to our spirit man which is enlightened by the Holy Spirit as opposed to our soulical man (the "I" in chapter seven) which is controlled by the physical world around us and our own mental evaluation of things, we will move into the same victory which Paul described in chapter eight verse six. Being directed by the Holy Spirit through our human spirit will bring us to a place of victory over the sinful nature that is inherent in our mortal existence. (Romans 8:1, Galatians 5:16) However, we must remember that it is our choice to live this way. Living and walking in the Spirit is a lifestyle, not just an experience. We do not automatically fall into all these blessings simply because we accept Jesus into our lives. We must make a determinate decision to follow the guidance of the Spirit. (Proverbs 3:5-7, Galatians 5:16-25, Romans 8:14)

We have a job to do, but we can't do it without the Holy Spirit. Although education, organization, and human talents are all beneficial, they cannot do the job. Like a carpenter without a hammer or a plumber without a wrench, we Christians will never complete the Great Commission which Jesus left with us if we do not have the Holy Spirit with us. (Matthew 28:19, Mark 16:15, Luke 24:47-48, Acts 1:8) In the same way we use an extension cord to operate a power tool some distance from the wall outlet, we must learn to rely upon the Holy Spirit to extend the power of God from heaven into our present situation.

I remember a little gray-haired man I once met in Madras, India. He had come there for an evangelism conference where he first learned about the baptism in the Holy Spirit. This little man had spent many years trying to witness in his little Hindu village, but had not yet won his first convert. After having moved into a new dimension of spiritual authority when he was filled with the Spirit at the conference, he returned to his home with a renewed confidence and faith. Upon his arrival, he met an old woman who had been gored by a water buffalo. Even though she was twisted and crippled from the attack, the evangelist asked if he could pray for her in the name of Jesus. She agreed, and he laid his hands on her and spoke with a boldness unlike anything he had ever experienced before – and he experienced results which he had never experienced before: her twisted body instantly straightened up! That day, he learned why Jesus had said that believers should treat the power of the Holy Spirit like the old American Express credit card commercial admonishes us, "Don't leave home without it!" (Luke 24:49)

I have found that living in the dimension of the Holy Spirit is an absolute "must" for a victorious Christian life. Time after time, it has been the Holy Ghost factor that has given me the winning edge. Once I was invited by a well-known evangelist to serve as his youth director. For a kid just out of college, this was a real honor and an open door for a great ministry. But something inside – the Holy Spirit – said, "Wait two weeks." So I asked for two weeks to pray before I made the decision. During those two weeks, the man was caught in adultery with a lady in Canada. Like dominos, other cases of adultery began to pop up all across the country. How wonderful it was that I was able to save my reputation by not becoming part of such an organization!

In other cases, the Holy Spirit has spoken through other individuals via the gifts of the word of knowledge or the word of wisdom to help me know how to direct my life. While working one summer in Yosemite National Park, I was approached for a full-time position. It was an absolute dream come true – living and ministering full-time in one of nature's wonderlands. It was toward the end of the summer, and I had to make a decision quickly as to whether I should accept the offer or return for my last semester of seminary. It was then that I met a minister who was vacationing in the park. Because of his unusual ministry of looking at individuals and giving them Bible verses that are God's directions or encouragements for them at the moment, some of the local believers coerced him to minister to them in a home fellowship. As we entered the park ranger's living room, I wound up seated next to the minister. He turned to me and said, "Young man, you have a decision to make within the next ten days. Don't you?" I replied in the affirmative and he responded that God would speak to me through Isaiah 30:20. Then he went on with the meeting. Flipping my Bible open, I found the indicated verse and read, "Thine eyes shall see thy teachers." Instantly I knew that I was not able to complete my studies by correspondence as I had considered because I had to be in class to see the teachers.

On another occasion, I was visiting a church in Wrightsville Beach, NC. As I walked in the door, I was welcomed by one of the ushers who grabbed me in a "Pentecostal bear hug" of a greeting. Since he was a very tall and rotund man, when he pulled me to himself, he actually picked me up off the floor. There I hang – suspended between heaven and earth – when suddenly the anointing of the Holy Spirit fell upon this man. He began to dance and spin in the Holy Spirit. As I was being whirled about in midair by this total stranger, he began to tell me my life story. He proclaimed that I was to go around the world to teach the gospel. My ears really perked up at that because I had never been out of the country except short excursions into Canada and Mexico! Since that time, I have literally traveled the globe to hold national teaching sessions to help establish the local believers in their Christian faith.

Probably the most dramatic exper
supernatural guidance through the Holy S
another of North Carolina's Atlantic coast k
organized a retreat for Christian studen'
several North Carolina campuses. The re
was planned as a teaching conference, yet a numʋꝋ. _
the participants wanted to use the time to do beach
evangelism. Tension began to rise as the students began
to split into two camps – those who wanted to evangelize
and those who wanted to be taught. Sensing the turmoil
in the air, I picked the top leaders of each group – three
from each side. Leading them to an attic room in the
ocean-side house we had rented for the weekend, I said,
"We're going to the Upper Room until the Holy Ghost falls
like He did on Pentecost." After a short season of prayer,
one young man began to prophesy. After a few sentences,
he abruptly stopped in mid-sentence. Across the room
another young man picked up the message, finished the
sentence, and added several more lines. But he, too,
stopped in mid-sentence. Again, the message was picked
up without missing a word and completed by another of
the participants in our prayer group. He also stopped in
mid-sentence. Again and again this happened until
everyone in the room had taken part in the prophetic word.
One prophecy, spoken by seven of us – bouncing back
and forth between leaders of two opposing sides of the
argument – confirmed that the original plan for a training
conference was God's plan for our weekend. The group
was brought into harmony and given excellent direction
through the Holy Spirit's gifts. To confirm the word, a
rainstorm blew in that evening and drenched the coastline
for our entire stay. No beach ministry could have occurred
after all!

We may often think that the gifts of the Spirit are for
supernatural use in church services and are possibly
restricted to the clergy only. However, God is interested

ery area of our lives and is eager to be involved in any
d every aspect. I believe that He wants us to learn to
use the gifts of the Spirit in our daily lives as well as in our
ministries. The passage in which the Apostle Paul
instructs the Ephesian church about being filled with the
Spirit leads directly into the section of his letter in which he
teaches on the family. (Ephesians 5:9-10)

The Lord has used the word of knowledge many
times to guide or protect me in my personal life. One such
experience was after I had taken my wife on her first
missionary trip. It had been a real struggle for her. Instead
of being with our little two-year old toddler on Mother's
Day, I was dragging her through the orphan-laden streets
of Calcutta, India. The next week was her birthday, but on
that day she was not to have a cake with candles and a
nice party. Instead, she would be stuck in the sand on a
jungle road surrounded by wild boars and other Sri Lankan
beasts. It seemed only fair that I reward her with at least
one nicety from her first missionary trip. When I learned
that one of my friends in Sri Lanka had become involved
in the trade of gemstones that are so splendid in that
country, I decided to arrange for her to have a nice
sapphire necklace and ring as appreciation gifts for her
endurance on the trip. They were beautiful, and she was
more than pleased – until they turned up missing when we
arrived home! I took the suitcase apart; I unfolded every
item of clothing we had packed; I looked under every piece
of furniture we had touched since returning home; I went
through the trash can and kitchen garbage piece by piece;
I even looked through the baby's diaper pail, opening each
disposable one by one! But still no necklace and ring!
Where in the world could they be? For sure, I had "left no
stone unturned." Finally, the jet lag began to take its toll,
and I stretched out on the sofa and succumbed to its
forces. I had actually slept for only about five minutes
when my mind was overtaken by a dream. In it I saw the

exact location of the missing jewelry. I leapt from the couch and began to look for my wife. Alas, she had left for the store; so, I began my nervous wait. Finally, she returned, and I met her at the door. She had barely made it across the threshold when I grabbed her purse and began to empty it. Almost too shocked to ask what was going on, she stood dumbfounded as I began to pull the lining out of the handbag. In the dream, I had seen the items inside the lining of the purse – and as I pursued my quest, I found them in the exact spot as in the dream! Apparently she had dropped them in the side pocket of her purse for safekeeping during the airplane trip. A tiny hole had allowed them to fall into the inner folds of the purse. No one had seen it – except God, and He willingly shared His secret with His beloved children through the gift of a word of knowledge.

On another occasion, the angel of death was cheated of the prize of taking my life in an automobile accident because my mother was directed by a supernatural word of knowledge. She rescued me from the snare of the trap just as the spring was tripped and the jaws were ready to devour me. The miracle of it is that she was hundreds of miles away. Driving from Washington, DC, to Delaware during rush hour one Friday afternoon, I found myself in bumper-to-bumper traffic racing along at nearly sixty miles per hour. As the flow of traffic moved from the open terrain to the vicinity of Baltimore, we suddenly encountered the congestion of major city traffic trying to merge into the freeway as they too joined the urban exodus for the summer weekend. Suddenly, the snarl of traffic brought us to a total standstill. Within seconds, our break-neck pace was brought to an idle. That is, except for the car behind me, whose driver seemed to be oblivious to the traffic jam. Still charging forward at an excessive speed, the car plowed into my little burgundy Mustang. My car was slammed into the car ahead of me that was, in turn, smashed into the one in front of it. Sustaining the full impact of this four-car collision, my sporty little car was instantly transformed into a giant metal accordion. It became a truly "compact car." I had to climb out the window to escape my prison of twisted metal and shattered glass. But through it all, I came out with only one minor injury – a cut under my chin that required five small stitches. But how was it that my mother figures into this rescue? In South Carolina, she suddenly was impressed to pray for me at the exact time of the accident!

I could go on and on, reciting stories such as the one of how the Lord woke me up early one morning and told me that that day was the day that a close family member was to come to Him. I convinced my wife to make a visit that day; and she did, indeed, lead her to the Lord – just days before she was admitted to the hospital with the disease which eventually took her life! Or the one about how I returned the favor on my mother's supernatural intercession for my life by praying for my son at the exact moment he was in what could have been a fatal automobile accident – I was not in church or even being "spiritual," rather I was half a world away, snorkeling in a lagoon on an island in the South Pacific.

The word of wisdom is similar to the word of knowledge, but it involves supernatural foreknowledge concerning the future. My favorite story about this gift happened in the life of one of my students who also raised cattle on his farm in Colorado. One year, an extended drought had plagued the state to the extent that no cattle ranchers were buying cows to raise, knowing that the added expense of feeding and watering them rather than allowing them to graze on the open range would eat up any profit they might hope to make and actually take them into the "red" for the year. When my student was praying about how to best position himself in the questionable cattle market, the Lord brought a Bible verse concerning rain to his mind. The verse even mentioned a certain month in which rains would come. Accepting that insight as a direction from God, he stocked his farm with cattle and expected the drought to break in time for them to have sufficient food and water to fatten up in time for market. At exactly the time mentioned in the verse he had trusted in, the rains came! Because so many other farmers had limited their stock that year, he got top dollar for his cattle and made a great profit while most of his neighbors barely broke even!

Discerning of spirits is another area in which the Lord may speak to us in our everyday lives. I was cleaning a large attic room of a house that we had just purchased. The building was empty, and I was all alone as I swept away years of dust. Suddenly, I felt an evil presence as I worked my way across the middle of the hardwood floor. Clutching the broom a little tighter, I looked around to locate the source of this unwelcome invader. My attention was drawn upward to the light fixture directly above my head. I noticed immediately that there was a sort of secret cubbyhole above the light where a horizontal platform for mounting the fixture had been suspended from the slanted ceiling. After locating a chair, I climbed up to investigate that mysterious secret compartment. Inside, I found the most horrible cache of pornographic literature imaginable. After removing the literature, the demonic presence left the room. I can only imagine how tormented a family could have been had someone without a sensitivity to the Holy Spirit purchased that house and moved their children into that attic bedroom. Thank God that He gives the gifts of the Holy Spirit to us to use in our daily lives as well as in our church ministry.

When it comes to the gifts of power, it is difficult to carefully discern the dividing line between the various manifestations. In the gift of faith God works on our behalf as a result of a supernatural ability to trust Him that He has placed inside of us. The working of miracles is when God supernaturally works through us to bring exponentially greater results when we exert our own human effort. Many times it is difficult to determine unquestionably when our actions are the "step of faith" it takes to prove that we really believe in God's promises and when those actions are the exertion of our human abilities which "prime the pump" for God's miraculous intervention. When healings come, it is difficult to unequivocally distinguish if they are the result of faith, miracles, or the gifts of healing. The only thing that really matters is that we are convinced that God does want to work supernaturally in our personal lives. Let me share a few examples of how God's supernatural intervention has come into our family's finances when we dared to believe God's promises and take action to demonstrate our trust in Him.

As newlyweds, my wife and I often struggled through on a shoe-string budget. At one point, we were down to only five dollars in our checking account and no cash in our wallets. We sat in our living room one evening calculating how we would make it through to the next payday. It was the time of the month for the newspaper boy to come and collect his five-dollar charge, and we knew that he would probably be arriving soon to ask for that last bit out of our checking account. When the doorbell rang, my wife whispered, "Don't answer it; it's probably the paper boy." I responded, "No, if we owe him, and we have it, I'm going to pay him." To our surprise and relief, it was not the paperboy coming to drain our account; instead, it was a neighbor with tears in his eyes proclaiming, "Here! God spoke to me to bring you this!" As he handed us a thirty-dollar check, we all rejoiced because no one had any way of knowing about our personal need except that it had been revealed supernaturally. The other amazing part of the story is that he had originally argued with the Lord about bringing us the money – assuming that we had no financial lack. Finally, he had conceded to make the visit with one condition – that if no one answered the door, he would know that it was not the Holy Spirit directing him to give us the blessing. Once we graduated from the "shoe-string" budget to what you might consider a "boot-lace" budget, the only thing that changed was the size of the miracles God continued to do in our lives.

Concerning the inspirational gifts of prophecy, speaking in tongues, and interpretation of tongues, it is always necessary to have godly words that fulfill the threefold functions of edification, exhortation, and comfort. (I Corinthians 14:3) I remember a conversation I had with Peggy before we were married. I had made a commitment of my love for her and devotion to her, but she had difficulty accepting it because previous boyfriends had made similar statements without heartfelt sincerity. Her response was, "Words are cheap," to which I immediately replied, "Not my words." It was a simple reply, but I believe that it was quickened by the Holy Spirit because it brought comfort to her, it strengthened or edified our relationship, and it encouraged or exhorted us to make the next step in our relationship – officially announcing our engagement.

It had been a long, exhausting night of counseling with a young couple who were bitterly enraged at each other. To hear her talk, it seemed that he was the worst husband to have ever walked the planet. Of course, hearing his side of the story would make you think that she was some sort of a she-devil and the very source of all their problems if not the root of evil all together! What made it worse was that they were missionaries – God's very mouthpieces in a pagan land! After several hours of listening to their enflamed accusations toward each other as all our futile attempts to counsel them fell on deaf ears, I suddenly turned to the husband and asked, "How much have you been praying in tongues lately?" He confessed that he had neglected his supernatural prayer language altogether for several months. I then turned to the wife and asked the same question. She also confessed to allowing the gift to lie dormant. We then laid hands on the couple and began to pray over them until they each broke forth in fluent heavenly languages. Before long, they were hugging and kissing as rivers of repentant tears poured from their eyes and rivers of Holy Ghost living water poured out of their innermost beings! Their lives, marriage, and ministry were renewed that night simply because they began to use the supernatural key to victory – their prayer languages.

At our house, we make a purposeful determination to pray in tongues on a daily basis because we believe the biblical promises that praying in the Spirit is the key to seeing that all things work together for our good (Romans 8:26-28) and that speaking in tongues strengthens us personally (I Corinthians 14:4) while building us up on our faith (Jude 20).

The Holy Spirit - Our Quarterback

The Apostle Paul introduces chapter twelve of I Corinthians with the admonition that we should not be ignorant of spiritual things. Although most translations use the word "gifts" in this sentence, that term is in italic indicating that it is not part of the original Greek text. Actually, Paul wants us to learn about more spiritual realities than just the gifts. In I Corinthians 12:7, Paul speaks of "manifestations of the Holy Spirit." The use of this term makes us keenly aware that he is not talking about human ability, but divine ability operating in these functions. The verses leading up to this passage suggest that the manifestations can be subdivided into three categories.

> *Now there are diversities of gifts, but the same Spirit. And there are differences of administrations, but the same Lord. And there are diversities of operations, but it is the same God which worketh all in all. But the manifestation of the Spirit is given to every man to profit withal. (I Corinthians 12:4-7)*

Gifts are given by the Holy Spirit. (I Corinthians 12:4) Administrations are given by Jesus, the Lord. (I Corinthians 12:5) Operations come from God. (I Corinthians 12:6) Paul goes on to list the specific functions within each category. These listings may not be all-inclusive in that we see other lists in other portions of scripture that seem to complete or augment the items enumerated here. The gifts of the Spirit are listed in I Corinthians 12:8-10. These are the supernatural abilities that we have already mentioned in other contexts. From Ephesians 4:11, we can understand that Jesus is in charge of placing individual believers into positions so that they can minister with the supernatural gifts that the Holy Spirit has placed inside of them. These individuals are identified as the administrations of the Lord in Paul's listing in I Corinthians 12:28-30. This list is certainly not exhaustive as we can readily see evangelists, pastors (Ephesians 4:11), deacons (I Timothy 3:8), and elders (Titus 1:5) are missing from the list – not to mention the fact that every believer is also endued with these spiritual gifts (Romans 12:3-8; I Corinthians 12:7, 12:11-20; Ephesians 4:16). The operations of God as discussed in I Corinthians 13:13 are faith, hope, and love; however, this list would unquestionably include all the qualities listed as the fruit of the spirit in Galatians 5:22-23. Even though these characteristics are defined as the fruit of the spirit, it is most likely that Paul's intention was that we would see them as the fruit that comes out of our human spirit rather than a supernatural manifestation of the Holy Spirit. Remembering what we have already learned about the lack of capitalization in the Greek New Testament and the fact that this fruit is directly contrasted with the works of the flesh (not the works of the devil), it seems logical that Paul had in mind the godly characteristic of a Christian's inner regenerated man. Correlating this thought with the words of Jesus that the Father is the husbandman who cultivates our lives to maximize our fruit production (John 15:1-2), we can readily see how that the Father is recognized as the member of the divine Godhead with the authority over the operations – or motivations – through which the ministers whom Jesus has appointed manifest the supernatural abilities that the Holy Spirit has dispersed to them. The emphasis of chapter thirteen is that each work done must be motivated by love – the very manifestation of the personality of God the Father Himself who is the personification of love. (I John 4:8)

Notice how Jesus had preannounced all this in the last discourse He had with His disciples after the Last

Supper.   He promised them that they would do
supernatural things — even things that exceeded His own
miracles.   He told them that the key would be the
indwelling of the full Trinity in their lives and that love would
be the determining factor to having this presence of God
in their lives.

> *Verily, verily, I say unto you, He that*
> *believeth on me, the works that I do shall*
> *he do also; and greater works than these*
> *shall he do; because I go unto my Father.*
> *And whatsoever ye shall ask in my name,*
> *that will I do, that the Father may be*
> *glorified in the Son.   If ye shall ask any*
> *thing in my name, I will do it.   If ye love*
> *me, keep my commandments.   And I will*
> *pray the Father, and he shall give you*
> *another Comforter, that he may abide with*
> *you for ever; Even the Spirit of truth;*
> *whom the world cannot receive, because*
> *it seeth him not, neither knoweth him: but*
> *ye know him; for he dwelleth with you, and*
> *shall be in you.   I will not leave you*
> *comfortless: I will come to you.   Yet a little*
> *while, and the world seeth me no more;*
> *but ye see me: because I live, ye shall live*
> *also.   At that day ye shall know that I am*
> *in my Father, and ye in me, and I in you.*
> *He that hath my commandments, and*
> *keepeth them, he it is that loveth me: and*
> *he that loveth me shall be loved of my*
> *Father, and I will love him, and will*
> *manifest myself to him.   Judas saith unto*
> *him, not Iscariot, Lord, how is it that thou*
> *wilt manifest thyself unto us, and not unto*
> *the world? Jesus answered and said unto*
> *him, If a man love me, he will keep my*

words: and my Father will love him, and we will come unto him, and make our abode with him. He that loveth me not keepeth not my sayings: and the word which ye hear is not mine, but the Father's which sent me. These things have I spoken unto you, being yet present with you. But the Comforter, which is the Holy Ghost, whom the Father will send in my name, he shall teach you all things, and bring all things to your remembrance, whatsoever I have said unto you. Peace I leave with you, my peace I give unto you: not as the world giveth, give I unto you. Let not your heart be troubled, neither let it be afraid. (John 14:12-27)

This promise of divine help was actualized in the lives of the first disciples. In addition to the numerous examples we could cite from the accounts recorded in Acts, at least two scriptures specifically say that God actively did His part:

And they went forth, and preached every where, the Lord working with them, and confirming the word with signs following. Amen. (Mark 16:20)

God also bearing them witness, both with signs and wonders, and with divers miracles, and gifts of the Holy Ghost, according to his own will? (Hebrews 2:4)

In fact, the reality of divine involvement is so preeminent that some authors have made the clever play on words, based on the that fact the prefix "co" means "with," that Jesus left us with a <u>co</u>mmission — not just a mission — because He was determined to be part of the team. As a matter of fact, this is exactly what Jesus was intending when He invited us to be yoked together with Him in His yoke. (Matthew 11:29-30) What an unbeatable team!

In truth, we do better to say that we are on God's team rather than suggesting that He is on our team. Paul clarified the order of significance of team members in I Corinthians 3:9 when he wrote, "For we are labourers together with God: ye are God's husbandry, ye are God's building." In Philippians 2:13, he made it crystal clear that any motivation and any ability to function was not from our side, but totally from God's provision, "For it is God which worketh in you both to will and to do of his good pleasure." In Romans 15:18, he spoke of what Christ had accomplished through him, and it was in Galatians 2:20 that he spelled out the same truth with unequivocal clarity when he penned the words, "I am crucified with Christ: nevertheless I live; yet not I, but Christ liveth in me: and the life which I now live in the flesh I live by the faith of the Son of God, who loved me, and gave himself for me."

In fact, God is much more interested in seeing us fulfill our mission than any of us as His team members are. He often takes the initiative to "get the ball in play" and then turns to His team members to bring in the score. The story of Cornelius in Acts chapter ten and the story of Saul of Tarsus in Acts chapter nine are great examples of this truth. Notice how Cornelius had a divine encounter and was given a message to go to Simon the tanner's house to look for a man named Simon Peter – even before Peter was made aware that he was a player in this particular game. The same thing happened to Ananias when God had pre-committed him to go on what seemed like a suicide mission to find Saul of Tarsus even before he was asked to join the match. Current history is also filled with similar stories.

The first personal experience of this nature happened when I was a college student back in the 1970s, during the hippie revolution when "sex, drugs, and rock and roll" was the mantra for the day. One day I picked up a young girl who was hitchhiking near the campus. She only needed a lift for a few blocks, but that short ride put her on the most exciting journey of her life — the road to heaven. When she got into my car, she made a comment about the "God loves you" decal on my dashboard. As I began to tell her about the plan of salvation, she shared her story. As an atheist, she had rejected everything anyone had ever shared with her about God or the need for her soul to be saved. However, while experimenting with LSD, she had remained "high" while all the others who were "tripping" with her had come "down." In her drug-induced state, the only explanation she could imagine was that she was dead while all the others were still alive. When she did eventually come "down," she said that something inside of her cried out, "Thank God, I'm alive." At that moment, she knew that she must have a soul and that there must be a God. That divine encounter had prepared her for the conversation I was to share with her that day.

The first time I encountered one of these divine "handoffs" in which a person who was totally unfamiliar with the Christian faith had a preparatory visitation occurred in India. When I walked into a Christian bookstore, the clerk pointed my attention to a picture of Jesus that hung in the front window and said that he wanted to tell me about what had just happened. A Hindu man had come into the store a few days before asking if he could meet the man in the picture. When the shopkeeper explained that it was a painting of a man who lived many years ago, the customer was perplexed, saying that he had seen the man in his dreams several nights in a row and that he knew he needed to meet him. When he saw the painting, he understood that his quest for this mystery man had finally been fruitful. The store clerk, of course, led this hungry soul to salvation.

The most dramatic story I have encountered came from the remote mountains of Nepal where one of my friends was doing door-to-door evangelism. One man he met in a very isolated mountain village had been having visions of the various Hindu gods. In fact, he had filled numerous volumes with handwritten narratives of all the stories and revelations he had received about these deities. Then one night, he had a vision in which he was directed that he would be given a revelation about a more powerful deity if he would destroy all the journals he had written about the lesser deities. When he burned the other logbooks, he began to have visions and dreams about another god that he had never learned about before. He wrote the stories and revelations about this new god, but didn't have a name for him – until my friend came to his hut and introduced him to Jesus and showed him that the same stories he was recording had already been written down almost two thousand years before!

A little old lady from our church in Indiana traveled into the hinterlands of the Philippines to share the gospel in the unreached villages. In one of these villages, she met a very elderly man who had lived far beyond the normal life expectancy of the people in his area. When Aunty Ruth shared the message of Jesus with the old man, he readily responded with the words, "So that's His name!" He explained that he already knew about this true God through dreams and visions, but had never had an opportunity to know who He was. Only a few days after Aunty introduced him to Jesus, the old man passed away.

Andrew Wommack, the president of the Bible college where I teach, tells the story of introducing himself to a receptionist at a business he was visiting. When she asked what business he was in, Andrew responded that he was a minister. Her next question was, "For whom?" When Andrew replied that he was a minister for Jesus Christ, she immediately interrupted, "Well, then you're the man!" Of course, he questioned her, "What man?" She answered by telling her story. As a Buddhist, she had been going through her religious rituals the night before but felt as if what she was doing was in vain. So she simply prayed, "God, I know that You are real, but I'm not sure who You are. Please show Yourself to me." Instantly, a ball of light invaded her room and a voice spoke to her, "Tomorrow, I'll send a man to tell you who I am." God personally took the divine initiative to reach this woman, but He left the job of scoring the point to one of His ministers. God was <u>working</u> <u>with</u> Andrew Wommack just as He did with the early disciples. (Mark 16:20)

Today, there are incredible stories like the ones I've just shared, mostly coming from nations behind the Quran Curtain where Muslim men and women are having supernatural dreams and visions that initiate their quest for the One True God. Because I had heard so many stories about these divine visitations, I decided to investigate a little and asked the audience when I was ministering in the country of Niger – which is almost one hundred percent Islamic – if any of them had had such supernatural dreams and visions. To my surprise almost one fourth of the congregation raised their hands!

God truly is taking the initiative. (John 14:6) He is even more adamant about the Great Commission than we are (II Peter 3:9), but He always passes the ball to His human team members to score the point. Knowing that God is the primary player on the team does take some of the pressure off of us because we realize that we don't have to do it on our own. At the same time, we still need to be vigilant to make our move when the ball is served into our court.

It is teamwork that makes the dream work. Notice that every time the Great Commission was given, Jesus was speaking to the whole group of His disciples. Additionally, it seems almost symbolic that we have to hear from each of the evangelists in order to understand this point; they are working together as a team to give us this truth. First Corinthians chapter twelve makes it unequivocally clear that these promises from God are not for individuals alone, but for the Body of Christ as a whole. If we want to fulfill God's plan in our lives and in the world, we must learn to work together as the church universal – as our Holy Spirit "quarterback" calls the moves.

> But all these worketh that one and the selfsame Spirit, dividing to every man severally as he will. For as the body is one, and hath many members, and all the members of that one body, being many, are one body: so also is Christ. For by one Spirit are we all baptized into one body, whether we be Jews or Gentiles, whether we be bond or free; and have been all made to drink into one Spirit. For the body is not one member, but many. If the foot shall say, Because I am not the hand, I am not of the body; is it therefore not of the body? And if the ear shall say, Because I am not the eye, I am not of the body; is it therefore not of the body? If the whole body were an eye, where were the hearing? If the whole were hearing, where were the smelling? But now hath God set the members every one of them in the body, as it hath pleased him. And if they were all one member, where were the body? But now are they many members, yet but one body. And the eye cannot say

unto the hand, I have no need of thee: nor again the head to the feet, I have no need of you. Nay, much more those members of the body, which seem to be more feeble, are necessary: And those members of the body, which we think to be less honourable, upon these we bestow more abundant honour; and our uncomely parts have more abundant comeliness. For our comely parts have no need: but God hath tempered the body together, having given more abundant honour to that part which lacked: That there should be no schism in the body; but that the members should have the same care one for another. And whether one member suffer, all the members suffer with it; or one member be honoured, all the members rejoice with it. Now ye are the body of Christ, and members in particular. (I Corinthians 12:11-27)

The Holy Spirit – Our Abiding Guide

Now concerning spiritual gifts, brethren, I would not have you ignorant. Ye know that ye were Gentiles, carried away unto these dumb idols, even as ye were led. Wherefore I give you to understand, that no man speaking by the Spirit of God calleth Jesus accursed: and that no man can say that Jesus is the Lord, but by the Holy Ghost. (I Corinthians 12:1-3)

When Paul introduced his discussion on the gifts of the Holy Spirit, he took what seems like a really abrupt detour by discussing the pagan practices that the people once participated in. It is not until we get to the famous love chapter (thirteen) that we are able to begin to piece together what must have been in his mind as he penned these words. Paul says that practicing the gifts of the Spirit without the motivation of love is like a tinkling cymbal or a sounding brass. To understand what he meant, we need to be aware of the pagan practices familiar to the Corinthian believers. The pagan temples of the time had bells that served the same function as the bells in Hindu temples of today. They were essentially doorbells to announce the arrival of a devotee to the demon spirits that inhabited the shrine. They also contained gongs much like the gongs found in present-day Buddhist temples, which also serve the purpose of awakening the demonic presence. Paul's evaluation of speaking in tongues outside the divine control of love was that it was nothing more than a demonic practice arousing evil spirits. It is because of the possibility of activating the wrong spiritual powers that the apostle felt it important to lay a foundation of understanding the difference between the demonic and the Holy Spirit.

Unfortunately, it doesn't take too much experience in Pentecostal and charismatic circles for one to encounter those who are doing things that certainly seem to be miraculous, but are actually motivated by demonic spirits rather than the Holy Spirit. Jesus Himself said that there will be those who will do miracles in His name without ever having known Him. (Matthew 7:22-23) Therefore, we must not be impressed simply because unusual or supernatural manifestations may occur.

In contrast, maturing Christians should be in the process of being changed daily from glory to glory (II Corinthians 3:18) and ever increasing in their spiritual capacity (Romans 1:17). My personal conclusion concerning spiritual manifestations is that I am not impressed by falling under the anointing unless you can also stand up with anointing for Jesus; nor am I excited by speaking in tongues unless you can also talk boldly about Jesus in your known language; I'm not interested in those people who lay hands on the sick unless they can also extend a helping hand to a hurting brother; and I have no attraction to folks who shake under the power of the Spirit unless they can also shake their neighborhood with the power of the Spirit. Quite honestly, I really don't believe that God is very impressed either.

Probably because they have seen some of the abuses and counterfeits that were labeled as the operations of the Holy Spirit, many Christians believe and teach that the operation of the gifts of the Spirit is not for the present age. They base their teaching on Paul's statement that prophecies will fail and tongues cease (I Corinthians 13:8) when the perfect one is come. (I Corinthians 13:10) Their interpretation usually follows the logic that the perfect one is the New Testament in that it was the completion of God's Word and, therefore, the perfect or complete thing that had to come so that all partial knowledge would be done away. In considering such an argument, I cannot help imagining a group of church elders in the year 96 AD. They have gathered around a desperately ill Christian brother and are just ready to do as they have been accustomed to doing – lay hands on the sick brother and see him miraculously healed. (Mark 16:18, James 5:14-15) Just as the head elder is opening his mouth to proclaim spiritual authority over the sickness (Matthew 10:1), a messenger bursts through the front door, panting with excitement. He interrupts the prayer session to announce that a parchment has just arrived from the last remaining apostle. John, who is exiled on the prison island of Patmos, has just managed to get the manuscript smuggled back to the believers on the mainland. The courier's hand quivered with excitement as he extended the document to the head elder. With the arrival of the Apocalypse, the congregation erupted into immeasurable elation – all except the deathly ill young man. Why could not the envoy have been just a few minutes later? If only the arrival of that copy of the final segment of the canon had been delayed a few precious minutes, he could have been healed. Now, however, he was destined to continue his suffering and go to an early grave. He had been cheated out of years of life and destined to extensive pain by the untimely arrival of the book of Revelation! How absurd!! There is no reasonable logic to the idea that God would withhold His blessings from His Body simply because the New Testament had been completed.

I was once at a conference of a Christian ministry that taught that the operation of the gifts of the Spirit was a thing of the past and even believed that it was only through demonic counterfeits that such manifestations could occur in these modern times. I used this convention as an occasion to research their teachings on the subject. Since there was a very well stocked book table displayed at the conference, I decided to browse through this plethora of readily available resources to see exactly when and how the supernatural gifts came to an end. One book said that it was with the completion of the book of Revelation. Another source stated that the pivotal event was the death of the last apostle; that added a few years. The next resource I consulted suggested that the gifts terminated at the end of the first century; again, a few more years were added. Another book gave the date as the end of the second century; this time, the date was stretched by a hundred years. Another volume I checked painted with a broad brush stroke, giving a range of somewhere in the third or fourth century! I shook my head as I walked away from the book display thinking, "Well, if you don't know when they stopped, how can you be sure that they really have passed away?" On the other hand, I could go through the annals of history and point to the operation of these gifts in every period of church history.

Those who oppose the present-day operation of the gifts say that these were just special impartations given to give the church a "jump start" to get it going. In light of this explanation, I ask just one simple question which – although it seems too elementary for a theological discussion – addresses a major issue: "If it takes a locomotive to get a train started, won't it also take a locomotive to get it to its destination?"

One last thought to consider on this point is that if the completion of the New Testament terminated the operation of the gifts, will the gifts continue in operation among the people groups who do not yet have the New Testament in their native language? If so, then there are vast regions of our world where these charismatic gifts can still operate in validity. If this is the case, then God must be playing favorites by allowing some of His family to enjoy such wonderful blessings as healings and miracles while the rest of us are denied these benefits.

And I will pray the Father, and he shall give you another Comforter, that he may abide with you for ever. (John 14:16)

The Holy Spirit – Maker of the Man and the Manifestation for the Mandate

The theme of the Holy Spirit keeps coming up time and again as we look at the history of the mission that Jesus left us of taking His gospel to the whole world. In the book of Acts, each expansion of the church was accompanied with a fresh move of the Holy Spirit. As we look through the centuries, we see people like St. Patrick who instilled an awareness for the necessity of the Holy Spirit in his followers and whole movements such as the Pietistic Movement that were characterized by an awareness of the presence of the Holy Spirit. From the very mission mandate itself through the first-century apostles to the twenty-first-century Pentecostals and charismatics, the move of the Holy Spirit is an unmistakable thread woven right into the fabric of missions.

Vinson Synan, Regent University professor and historian of the Pentecostal movement, estimates that more than one fourth of the world's Christians are Pentecostal or charismatic. He said that, of the almost two billion people who profess the Christian faith, over half a billion of them are charismatic or Pentecostal. It has been estimated that twenty-three percent of Christians in America have experienced the Pentecostal gifts of the Holy Spirit. Among Catholics, it is estimated that about half a million practice speaking in tongues and that almost ten million have had this experience since the charismatic movement began within the Catholic Church in the 1970s. Synan points to South Korea as an example of how the faith has impacted a whole nation. Thirty percent of the population is Christian, making Christianity the largest faith group in the nation, and about sixty percent of all Korean Christians are Pentecostal.

The worldwide impact of the Pentecostal movement is an indication that we are living in the end times since the Bible prophesies that a worldwide inundation of the Holy Spirit's presence is a sign of the generation that is to close out human history as we know it.

> *And it shall come to pass in the last days, saith God, I will pour out of my Spirit upon all flesh: and your sons and your daughters shall prophesy, and your young men shall see visions, and your old men shall dream dreams: And on my servants and on my handmaidens I will pour out in those days of my Spirit; and they shall prophesy. (Acts 2:17-18, also Joel 2:28-29)*

Since we also know that one of the most significant signs of the end time is that the gospel will be preached to all nations (Matthew 24:14), we can equate these two prophetic signs and see that they will occur together in the end times. Not only is an outpouring of the Holy Spirit prophetically associated with worldwide evangelism, there actually seems to be a cause-and-effect relationship.

Unfortunately, there is still resistance among many denominational mission groups. I remember one couple who were in seminary with me. Even though they had prepared themselves fully for an appointment by their denominational missions board, they were rejected because they practiced speaking in tongues. I also remember hearing of one evangelical mission leader who requested prayer concerning the explosive growth of a "cult" group in his area: the culprit – the Assemblies of God! One very large denominational mission board has long held a strong stance against charismatics serving under their authority on the field. Their present regulation for missionaries who speak in tongues is almost identical to their statement concerning homosexuality. However, there are winds of change even there. When requests were made that the denomination include a statement on speaking in tongues in their statement of faith, criticism of the anti-tongues position was accompanied with predictions of a mass exodus, especially among black congregations, if the denomination banned speaking in tongues.

As we have already noted, Jesus had four different relationships with the Holy Spirit. He was born of the Spirit (Matthew 1:20), He was filled with the Spirit and led by the Spirit (Luke 4:1), and He was empowered by the Holy Spirit (Luke 4:14). We, too, need to have the Holy Spirit working in our lives in all these dimensions. According to the conversation Jesus had with Nicodemus in John chapter three, we must be born of the Spirit to enter the kingdom of heaven. Being filled with the Holy Spirit is such a necessity that Jesus made the requirement like having an American Express card, telling His disciples not to leave home without it. (Luke 24:49) In Romans chapter eight verse fourteen, Paul insisted that being led by the Spirit is a hallmark characteristic of being a child of God. Jesus felt that being empowered of the Holy Spirit was so important that He made it the topic of His last conversation with His followers. (Acts 1:8)

In John 16:7, Jesus said that it was expedient for us that He should go away because unless He left, the Holy Spirit could not come. The word "expedient" means fitting or proper. In other words, it was a good thing for Jesus to leave, and the reason that it was good for Him to leave was so that the Holy Spirit could come. What is the advantage of having the Holy Spirit? As we are already aware, the first thing that Jesus said was that He would work in conviction or cross-examination. (John 16:8) Cross examination is when the attorney asks questions about the same event in a way as to elicit a whole new set of answers and a whole new way of looking at the issue. This is what Jesus did when He wrote in the sand as the woman was being tried for adultery. The power of having our lives cross examined by the Spirit is that we are always ensured that we are seeing all the issues from God's eternal perspective rather than only through our limited viewpoint. "For as the heavens are higher than the earth, so are my ways higher than your ways, and my thoughts than your thoughts." (Isaiah 55:9) The wonderful promise is that God has given us the Holy Spirit as a constant proofreader to point out our mistakes before they become serious errors.

We should also remember that Paul spoke of the Spirit only four times in the first seven chapters of Romans, but twenty times in chapter eight alone. He ended chapter seven in defeat, but moved into chapter eight in great victory. The progression of the book in chapters one through five set the theological stage for salvation, chapter six gave the salvation experience, and chapter seven described the attempt to live one's post-salvation existence in one's own human power. This chapter is full of the first person pronoun, "I." Some Bible scholars try to suggest that Paul may have had an "eye" problem; this theory cannot be proven, but it is certain from this chapter that he definitely had an "I" problem. In chapter eight, Paul gave his victorious answer to his dilemma through the power of the Holy Spirit. He concluded in chapters nine through sixteen by giving practical applications of these truths to our Christian lives.

As early as verse six of chapter seven, Paul suggested that our ability to live a victorious Christian life was through the power of the Holy Spirit. "But now we are delivered from the law, that being dead wherein we were held; that we should serve in newness of spirit, and not in the oldness of the letter." However, it wasn't until the first couple verses of chapter eight that he spelled out how the

Holy Spirit would help us live above the controlling power of sin. "There is therefore now no condemnation to them which are in Christ Jesus, who walk not after the flesh, but after the Spirit. For the law of the Spirit of life in Christ Jesus hath made me free from the law of sin and death." In Galatians 5:16-25, he makes it even plainer, "This I say then, Walk in the Spirit, and ye shall not fulfil the lust of the flesh...If we live in the Spirit, let us also walk in the Spirit." What a promise! It doesn't matter whether you speak in tongues if you still lie in English or whether you fall out in the Spirit if you still stand in the way of sinners when you get up! The Holy Spirit is here to help us overcome our weaknesses in prayer (Romans 8:26) and to strengthen and empower us (I Corinthians 14:4, Jude 20, Acts 1:8).

As we mentioned in another context, Jesus called the Holy Spirit the Spirit of truth. (John 14:17, 15:26, 16:13) He went on to add that the Holy Spirit would impart to us all that He learned from Jesus and that the result would be that He would reveal things that are to come. Jesus is the truth (John 14:6; Revelation 3:7, 14; 19:9, 11; 21:5; 22:6), but it is the Holy Spirit who reveals Him to us. Paul made a special point of praying for the believers at Ephesus that they would have the advantage of the revelatory power of the Holy Spirit because he knew that it was only through the Holy Spirit's enlightenment that we would ever know what power resides inside us through having Christ alive in us. "[I] cease not to give thanks for you, making mention of you in my prayers; That the God of our Lord Jesus Christ, the Father of glory, may give unto you the spirit of wisdom and revelation in the knowledge of him: The eyes of your understanding being enlightened; that ye may know what is the hope of his calling, and what the riches of the glory of his inheritance in the saints, And what is the exceeding greatness of his power to us-ward who believe, according to the working of his mighty power." (Ephesians 1:16-19) Remember how he paraphrased the prophet

Isaiah, "Eye hath not seen, nor ear heard, neither have entered into the heart of man, the things which God hath prepared for them that love him," (I Corinthians 2:9) and then immediately added, "But God hath revealed them unto us by his Spirit: for the Spirit searcheth all things, yea, the deep things of God." (verse 10) Even the great prophet Isaiah didn't have a clue as to all the victories we can experience when we are led by the Holy Spirit's wisdom and revelation – the truth of Christ.

Probably the next most important advantage of having the Holy Spirit in our lives is that we can manifest the fruit of the Spirit. (Galatians 5:22-23) These qualities help us show forth the personality of God to a godless generation. Just as a fruit tree laden with luscious fruit attracts all living things from bacteria to bumblebees to humans, so a spiritually ripe life attracts the attention of even the most skeptical of our society. If we lift up Jesus through our lives, we will certainly attract notice. (John 12:32) In the same way that we are not attracted to an apple tree until it has fruit on it, people are not attracted to us until we start to bear the fruit of the spirit.

Another really important aspect is that He gives us assurance in our prayers and decisions. (Romans 8:26-28) The Holy Spirit enhances our ability to recall the promises and instructions of the Lord – powerful tools that help us deal with our daily struggles and decisions. (John 16:26) He is also called the "Comforter," a title signifying that He will give us the tranquility necessary to live peaceably and make calm decisions. (John 16:7-11) Additionally, He gives us boldness in our witnessing and lives in general. (Acts 4:31) On the top of the list, as far as I'm concerned, is His guidance – especially in life's important decisions, but in our daily lives as well. (John 16:13) Of course, we must not overlook the fact that His main objective is to glorify Jesus. (John 16:14) It is the Holy Spirit who sees that the love of God is implanted into our hearts (Romans 5:5) and that the kingdom of God is birthed inside us (Romans 14:17). The Holy Spirit declares the fact that we have been adopted by God. (Romans 8:16)

One marked difference in the life of a Spirit-filled believer is that he is given the ability to operate in the gifts of Spirit – the gifts of revelation, the gifts of power, and the gifts of inspiration that we have previously discussed. (I Corinthians 12:8-10) Through the manifestation of these supernatural abilities, we are able to demonstrate to the unbelieving world around us that God is still very much alive.

But by now, you must be wondering if I've forgotten that I'm addressing the issue of effecting a world-wide harvest of souls for the kingdom of God. No, I haven't forgotten – and I think that just one simple statement will help bring all that we just covered back into focus in the context of missions: missions is not just about the mandate; it's also about the man. The power of the Holy Spirit in our lives makes us into the people we need to be in order for us to be the missionaries God wants us to be.

In a previous chapter, we noticed that the twelve men who followed Jesus were almost always called "disciples" in the gospels, but became "apostles" in the book of Acts. This name change signified the radical change that occurred in their lives when they were empowered by the Holy Spirit on the Day of Pentecost. But this wasn't the end of the story, for the Holy Spirit kept showing up and empowering more and more believers. (Acts 4:31, 8:17, 9:17, 10:44, 19:6) Of course, this continued outpouring of the Spirit was of no surprise since Peter had promised it in his very first sermon on the Day of Pentecost, "I will pour out of my Spirit upon all flesh...For the promise is unto you, and to your children, and to all that are afar off, even as many as the Lord our God shall call." (Acts 2:17-39) Are you called of God? If so, you can also be anointed and become an apostle as well as a disciple. Since the words "apostle" and "missionary" both mean "a sent one," it is obvious that the indwelling of the Holy Spirit is a real necessity in the life of a sent out missionary. We have a job to do, but we can't do it without the Holy Spirit.

In order to understand what the Bible says about this supernatural phenomenon, let's start in Hebrews – a book which doesn't even mention speaking tongues: "For when for the time ye ought to be teachers, ye have need that one teach you again which be the first principles of the oracles of God; and are become such as have need of milk, and not of strong meat." (Hebrews 5:12) The Greek wording used in this verse literally means to learn ones ABCs. We can learn our ABCs concerning speaking in tongues by seeing that the gift is Available for us, that it has many Benefits, and that there are Conditions for its use.

In Luke 11:11-13, we find the very words of Jesus Himself, telling us that the gift of the Holy Spirit (including speaking with tongues) is a present that the Heavenly Father will willing give to His children. In Mark 16:17, Jesus added that this gift was readily available to all who would believe. Notice that the promise wasn't to pastors, elders, saints, or people in any specific time period; it was to all who would believe. Remember Peter's declaration on the Day of Pentecost that this gift of the Holy Spirit was for the people present, their children, and to all that are afar off – even as many as the Lord our God shall call. (Acts 2:39)

As wonderful as the gift of speaking in tongues may be, there are certain conditions set forth for proper use of this gift. Paul said in I Corinthians 14:15 that we should pray in the understanding as well as in the Spirit. In terms of the public use of tongues in a service, we must remember that we don't have to give a message in every service. In I Corinthians 14:19, Paul stressed the importance of speaking understandable messages in a known tongue rather than supernatural messages in tongues in a church service. First Corinthians 14:26 asks a question, "How is it then, brethren? when ye come together, every one of you hath a psalm, hath a doctrine, hath a tongue, hath a revelation, hath an interpretation?" and then gives the answer, "Let all things be done unto edifying." Many people feel that they must speak out any time they sense the presence of the Holy Spirit; however, I Corinthians 14:32 clearly teaches that the spirits of the prophets are subject to the prophets. In other words, we can decide if we are going to speak out or remain silent. The scripture also teaches that there should not be any message given unless there is an interpreter present. (I Corinthians 14:28) The interpreter also functions under a supernatural gift just as the one who speaks in tongues.

With the proper understanding of and the proper use of the power and qualities of the Holy Spirit, we can go forth as missionaries, sent out not only by our supporters but also by the personal touch of God Himself! Many Christians speak of trying to witness or minister as getting out of their "comfort zone." However, it is important to remember what Jesus said in John 14:26 – the Holy Spirit is our Comforter – and what David said in Psalm 139:7 – that there is nowhere we can go to get away from the Holy Spirit. If the Comforter goes with us everywhere we go, then it is impossible to be outside our "comfort zone"! This may seem like a novel way of thinking about things, but the truth is that Jesus expressed the same truth when He gave us the Great Commission. One common characteristic in each of these four different encounters is that a divine presence is promised as we respond to His mandate. Matthew 28:20 states, "Lo, I am with you alway, even unto the end of the world." Mark 16:20 records, "And they went forth, and preached everywhere, the Lord working with them, and confirming the word with signs following." Luke 24:49 says, "Behold I send the promise of my Father upon you." Acts 1:8 confirms that it is after they were to receive the Holy Ghost that they would have the power to be witnesses. The entire Trinity has promised to be involved with the believer who responds to the call upon his life. Jesus committed Himself to be with us; the Father has extended a promise of filling us with His Spirit; and the Holy Spirit has obligated Himself to empowering our witness. The Trinity's presence in the ministry of a called witness results in signs and wonders that confirm the words of that witness.

Missions is not only about a mandate and a man; it is also about manifestation. The consistent biblical pattern of evangelism is that men of God under a mandate from Him are to manifest His supernatural power to their unbelieving generation. Miraculous acts at the hands of Daniel resulted in empire-wide decrees from the ruling monarchs themselves that the entire population must reverence the God of Daniel. (verses 4:1-37, 6:25-27) When Jesus sent His disciples out, He commanded them to accompany their proclamation of the kingdom with demonstration of its presence. "Go preach saying, 'The kingdom of heaven is at hand.' Heal the sick, cleanse the lepers, raise the dead, cast out devils: freely ye have received, freely give." (Matthew 10:7-8) He added that even the citizens of Sodom would have repented had they been presented with a message confirmed with manifestations. (Matthew 10:15, 11:23-24, Mark 6:11, Luke 10:12) When He gave them the Great Commission, Jesus ordered the disciples to remain in Jerusalem until they were endued with the power of the Holy Spirit so that they would be able to confirm their message with signs and wonders. (Luke 24:49, Mark 16:17) The book of Acts records abundant examples of miraculous acts resulting in mass conversions: supernatural tongues on the day of

Pentecost (Acts 2:7-11), the healing of the lame man at the temple gate (Acts 3:1-9), miraculous healings and deliverances in Samaria (Acts 8:6-8), the raising of Dorcas from the dead (Acts 9:40-41), an angelic visit to Cornelius (Acts 10:3), and Paul's miraculous protection from a venomous snake bite and the healing of Publius' father on the island of Malta (Acts 28:3-9). In fact, the Apostle Paul declared that having signs and wonders in conjunction with his preaching was his *modus operandi* and that this combination of miracle and message had allowed him to fully saturate his targeted region. "Through mighty signs and wonders, by the power of the Spirit of God; so that from Jerusalem, and round about unto Illyricum, I have fully preached the gospel of Christ...But now having no more place in these parts, and having a great desire these many years to come unto you." (Romans 15:19-23) In his letter to the Corinthian church, he emphasized that he had come to them with the power of God as well as with God's powerful message. "And my speech and my preaching was not with enticing words of man's wisdom, but in demonstration of the Spirit and of power." (I Corinthians 2:4) Perhaps his ministry in this particular city was distinctly marked with miraculous signs and wonders because it followed immediately upon the heels of a rather unfruitful ministry in Athens where Paul seemed to rely on his human intellect and philosophical arguments rather than the miracle ministry that characterized his evangelism in other venues.

However, we should not place all the credit for the effectiveness of ministry on signs and wonders alone. In I Thessalonians 1:5, Paul made one simple statement that reveals five distinct elements in his approach to ministry – five different ways to manifest the Lord.

For our gospel came not unto you in word only, but also in power, and in the Holy Ghost, and in much assurance; as ye know what manner of men we were among you for your sake.

The first key he mentioned was the Word. Here he is speaking of the gospel message that has been confirmed and proven through the scriptures and then presented within a biblical context. In this regard, we must remember that Jesus described two very important elements in His parable about sowing seed – the seed and the soil into which it was sown. When He explained the parable, Jesus told us what the seed was and spelled out the significance of each of the four soils. Paul had a true desire to see people saved and he made a deliberate attempt to relate the gospel to them in a way that they would find relative and palatable. "To the weak became I as weak, that I might gain the weak: I am made all things to all men, that I might by all means save some." (I Corinthians 9:22) Like the Greeks with the Trojan horse and David at the watercourses of Jerusalem (II Samuel 5:7-8), the apostle looked for a way to get inside his target audience's defenses before he released his assault. In many cases, his subjects didn't even know what had hit them until they were fully in the grasp of the gospel.

Paul's second key was power. All we need is a quick review of the book of Acts to see that his ministry was indeed accompanied with miraculous events. (Acts 13:11, 16:16-18, 19:11, 20:9-10, 28:3-6) Next, Paul mentioned the Holy Ghost. In that the operation of the gifts seems to have been his topic in the previous category, we must interpret this reference to suggest a fuller meaning of the operation of the Holy Spirit in the believer's life. Turning to his letter to the Galatians, we see at least two areas where the Holy Spirit's influence must be evidenced in a believer's life and ministry. The first is in chapter five verses sixteen and eighteen: walking in and being led by the Spirit. Such Holy Spirit orchestrated movement is not only vitally important to the success of our personal lives and the productivity of our ministries; it may also make the difference between life and death. As Paul mentioned in the Galatian passage, the fatally destructive works of the flesh will overcome us unless we walk in the Spirit. In addition to the example we have already examined in how the apostle was directed away from Asia toward a fertile ministry in Europe through the Holy Spirit's direction, it would be good to remember how the inner voice of the Holy Spirit warned Paul of the impending danger into which his ship was to sail. (Acts 27:10) The other Holy Spirit quality that Paul discusses in Galatians chapter five is the fruit of the Spirit listed in verses twenty-two and twenty-three. Just as no one cares for a barren tree that does not produce fruit, people will not be attracted to our lives or ministries unless we manifest the fruit of the Spirit.

Paul followed with the quality of assurance. Even without an examination of some of the key biblical injunctions concerning assurance (Isaiah 32:17, Acts 17:31, Colossians 2:2, Hebrews 6:11, 10:22), we can recognize from the natural world that we never want to believe what someone is saying if we don't feel that he really believes it himself. Paul was persuaded of the validity of his message (Romans 8:38, 14:14, II Timothy 1:12) and admonished his disciples to be fully persuaded concerning their faith (Romans 14:5).

Allow me interject a little personal story at this point. A dear friend of mine in California was diagnosed as having an advanced case of the most aggressive strain of cancer. Her doctor was so concerned because of the rapid growth of this malignancy that he advised her to leave his office and go directly to the airport and book the first flight available to a certain clinic in Texas that was the only facility able to treat this form of cancer. He told her that the time she would waste going home to pack a suitcase would be critical considering the aggressive nature of her malady. The doctor was totally certain that his diagnosis was correct because he had had it confirmed by ninety doctors who worked under him at a major medical facility. Outside the doctor's office, my friend's husband asked if she wanted to go directly to the airport as she had been advised. Her response was that she first wanted to go to the church in accordance with James 5:14-15, "Is any sick among you? let him call for the elders of the church; and let them pray over him, anointing him with oil in the name of the Lord: And the prayer of faith shall save the sick, and the Lord shall raise him up." Their pastor called all the elders of the church together for a special prayer meeting and laid hands on my friend; however, she could sense doubt behind their prayer "of faith." One of them made the comment that when we get to heaven we will all be totally healed and have perfect bodies. That, of course, was a true report; but it was not a good report (Philippians 4:8) for a woman who was asking God to heal her while she was still here on earth! After leaving the church office, she told her husband that she could hear what they were saying with their lips but could also read what they were thinking by looking at their eyes, faces, and body language – and the two did not agree. She told him, "These people are not going to heal me; they are going to kill me! Please get me to a place where people really believe what they say!" When he promised to take her anywhere an airplane could fly, she asked to go to Indiana to be with my wife and me. They flew out on the next flight, and I arranged for special prayer by two great apostles – our pastor, Dr. Lester Sumrall, and the pastor of the world's largest congregation, Dr. Yonggi Cho. She then spent the next three days in our home and received a constant diet of faith-filled words that came with confidence out of our hearts, not just words out of our heads. My wife and I did nothing but reinforce the promises of God's Word concerning healing. When our friend did eventually make it to the clinic, the doctor refused to admit her because he couldn't find even a trace of cancer in her body! Assurance made a life-and-death difference in her case. Remember that her doctor told her that she didn't even have time to pack a suitcase? Well, that was over twenty-five years ago. Imagine how may suitcases she has packed in that quarter of a century

Character is the fifth key that Paul used to open the city of Thessalonica to the gospel. In our Thessalonian passage, he called it his "manner of man." To get a definition of this term, we can turn to his farewell to the Ephesian church where again he used this same expression and gave a rather lengthy explanation. The purity of his motives and the unselfishness of his service permeate the speech and testify to the quality of life he lived before the people. Who he was backed up what he said. As the old expression goes, he walked the walk as well as talked the talk. Another couplet reminds us that people don't care what you know unless they know that you care. Our personal character is likely the most powerful force in communicating to the world we wish to win for Christ. After all, many more people will read our lives than will ever read our tracts.

> And when they were come to him, he said
> unto them, Ye know, from the first day that
> I came into Asia, after what manner I have
> been with you at all seasons, Serving the
> Lord with all humility of mind, and with
> many tears, and temptations, which befell
> me by the lying in wait of the Jews: And
> how I kept back nothing that was
> profitable unto you, but have shewed you,
> and have taught you publickly, and from
> house to house, testifying both to the

Jews, and also to the Greeks, repentance toward God, and faith toward our Lord Jesus Christ...Wherefore I take you to record this day, that I am pure from the blood of all men. For I have not shunned to declare unto you all the counsel of God...Therefore watch, and remember, that by the space of three years I ceased not to warn every one night and day with tears...I have coveted no man's silver, or gold, or apparel. Yea, ye yourselves know, that these hands have ministered unto my necessities, and to them that were with me. (Acts 20:18-34)

I guess this last statement brings us back to the three essentials in missions: mandate, man, and manifestation. With these three elements in proper order, we can win our world!!!

The Holy Spirit - Revealer of Mysteries

I will begin this chapter by begging your indulgence because I want to speculate on some concepts that are not specifically spelled out in the scriptures, but I believe that we can connect the dots without any real violation to reason or the sanctity of the text. My concern here is to explore role of the Holy Spirit in the transformation of Saul of Tarsus into the Apostle Paul.

We know that Saul was an excellent student of the Word of God in that he studied under the most notable rabbi of his day. (Acts 22:3) His experience on the Road to Damascus threw him into a total "tailspin" in that this encounter totally contradicted everything that he "knew" and believed. In his brain, Saul was totally convinced that Jesus was the greatest blasphemer, heretic, and charlatan that ever lived; however, his heart yelled out that Jesus was Lord even before he knew who it was that he had encountered in that blinding light. (Acts 9:5) We also know that once he was converted on the Road to Damascus and then baptized and filled with the Holy Spirit under the ministry of Ananias (Acts 9:17) he spent the following three years in Arabia without any further contact with Christians – especially those who could have taught him the truth of the gospel (Galatians 1:16-17). In essence, he went into the Arabian desert with his head spinning with questions and came back out of that desert with answers of such clarity that his explanation of the gospel has changed the world. This definitive revelation of the gospel was what transformed him from the rabbi of Tarsus to the preeminent apostle of the faith. Since we weren't in the Arabian desert with him, we can only speculate as to how he came by such revolutionary illuminations since his previous knowledge was totally based on the rabbinic interpretations of the Old Testament – ideas that he literally defined as dung. (Philippians 3:8) In II Corinthians

12:7-9, Paul speaks of the revelations that he had received and says that they were so abundant (in significance as well as in quantity) that the devil assigned a special messenger to torment him because of these insights. Because of the abundance of his revelations, Satan felt it necessary to send a messenger to harass him in an attempt to keep the apostle from being exalted or recognized as an authority. Obviously the enemy knew that such a clear presentation of the gospel would literally destroy any possible leverage he would have against the Christian faith. Elsewhere, Paul described those revelations as mysteries that had been disclosed to him and even added that these mysteries were truths that had been hidden throughout the ages – essentially waiting for him to unravel them: the mystery which was kept secret since the world began (Romans 16:25), the wisdom of God in a mystery, even the hidden wisdom, which God ordained before the world unto our glory (I Corinthians 2:7), and the mystery which hath been hid from ages (Colossians 1:26).

Perhaps – and this is the point where I stretch the line pretty far between the two dots – this revelation came to him through speaking in tongues and the accompanying gift of prophecy. Although there is no reference to when he began the practice of praying in tongues, we do know that the apostle was an avid tongues speaker. (I Corinthians 14:18) It is likely that he could have begun the practice of speaking in tongues as soon as he was filled with the Holy Spirit since this seems to be a biblical pattern – the believers in the Upper Room on the Day of Pentecost (Acts 2:4), Cornelius and his household (Acts 10:45-46), the disciples in Ephesus (Acts 19:6), and most likely the believers in Samaria (Acts 8:17-19). We also assume that Paul was referring to himself when he wrote of a person who was caught up into paradise, and heard unspeakable words, which it was not lawful for a man to utter. (II

Corinthians 12:4) Notice the similarity of thought when he speaks of this experience being unutterable and the way he described speaking in tongues in Romans 8:26 as being in unutterable groanings. If all these dots do indeed connect, we can conclude that Paul spent much of the time that he was isolated in Arabia speaking in tongues so that he could get the revelation of the mysteries of God in his spirit, and then he pressed into prophecy so that the unspeakable truths in his heart became compensable to his mind in such a clear way that he could pen them to present a clear legacy of gospel truth for generations to come.

The reason I feel that Paul's avenue into these revelations was through speaking in tongues is his statement in I Corinthians 14:2, "For he that speaketh in an unknown tongue speaketh not unto men, but unto God: for no man understandeth him; howbeit in the spirit he speaketh mysteries." Some theologians feel that speaking in tongues is nothing more than some sort of emotional high that those who practice it use in order to escape reality. They say that the words themselves mean nothing and that the only value that the practice may bring is simply the euphoria that the speaker may experience for the few minutes that he or she is disconnected from the real world. On the contrary, speaking in tongues is not an escape from reality; rather, it is a divine connection to a level of reality that can only be approached through a supernatural connection.

The first thing that I'd like for us to notice in this verse is how Paul describes what happens when a person speaks in tongues – "in the spirit, he speaks mysteries." With this explanation, it might be easy to understand why some people would discredit the practice, saying that speaking mysteries, or unintelligible ideas, is pointless. But before we jump to any rash conclusions, it is important for us to remember that there is a radical difference between the two words "unintelligible" and "unintelligent." Just because something is inexpressible does not mean that it is senseless. In fact, the Bible gives us two powerful examples of things that are considered unspeakable, yet to be treasured – the joy of knowing Christ (I Peter 1:8) and the grace of God we experience in salvation through Christ (II Corinthians 9:14-15).

The second area that we should focus on in this verse is the fact that what is being spoken is defined as mysteries. Some might immediately respond that there is no point in focusing on things that are unsolvable – or, at least, unsolved. But exactly the opposite is actually true. To understand this point, let's take a look at some of the things that the Bible describes as mysteries:

> The kingdom of heaven or God (Matthew 13:11, Mark 4:11, Luke 8:10)
> Christ and God (I Corinthians 4:1; Colossians 2:2, 4:3)
> God's will (Ephesians 1:9)
> Christ and the church (Ephesians 5:32)
> The gospel (Ephesians 6:19)
> The faith in a pure conscience (I Timothy 3:9)
> Godliness (I Timothy 3:16)
> Christ in you, the hope of glory (Colossians 1:27)

Certainly no one would dare to say that any of these subjects is unworthy of consideration and meditation! In that case, it does seem advantageous to speak of them in our prayers – even in prayers that are unintelligible to the natural mind.

The third area of focus that I would like to consider in this verse is that the tongues speaker is described as speaking to God rather than man. Now, let's apply a bit of basic logic to the matter at hand. Let's say that you were having trouble with your car, would you go ask the local grocer how to get it working properly? Obviously not – you'd go to the automobile mechanic. Why? Because he is the one who knows the answer to the mystery of why your car is not working properly. Need I really take the space on this page to draw out the analogy that it is the all-wise God to whom we need to address these mystery issues? Since it is obvious that we must have an understanding of God, Jesus, the gospel, God's will, His kingdom, and what exactly it means that Christ is in us, it is only logical that we need to address these issues to the proper authority and in the proper way. Romans 8:26-28 explains exactly how this happens.

> *Likewise the Spirit also helpeth our infirmities: for we know not what we should pray for as we ought: but the Spirit itself maketh intercession for us with groanings which cannot be uttered. And he that searcheth the hearts knoweth what is the mind of the Spirit, because he maketh intercession for the saints according to the will of God. And we know that all things work together for good to them that love God, to them who are the called according to his purpose.*

The Holy Spirit knows that we don't even know how to address the Lord properly concerning these mysteries; therefore, He assists us by praying with words that we would never be able to imagine, framing questions that we would not be able to construct. And He does this in tongues. Because He knows exactly what is in our hearts (our unintelligible – but not unintelligent – questions and concerns) and also knows the exact will of God (as opposed to our limited comprehension of it), He presents our requests in the exact manner that renders the wonderful result of having everything work out just perfectly on our behalf! But as wonderful as that may be, it seems that there may be even more in this verse – the involvement of the very Son of God, Jesus Christ. Notice that the verse says that the one making intercession is the one who knows the mind of the Spirit – apparently someone other than the Holy Spirit Himself. Of course, we have to be cautious before we jump to conclusions because – as we have already discussed – Greek at the time the Bible was penned didn't use capital letters. Therefore, the word "Spirit" could originally have been written with a small letter, indicating the human spirit rather than the Holy Spirit. In this case, the word "mind" would have to be understood not so much as the brain but the thinking process. If this is the case, then Paul is saying that the Holy Spirit knows what's going on in our spirits as we pray those unintelligible words, and He translates our requests to God in intelligible words. However, if we retain the capitalization, the verse is definitely speaking of someone other than the Holy Spirit since it is illogical to say that the Holy Spirit knows His own mind. In that we know that Jesus lives eternally to make intercession for us (Hebrews 7:25), the only reasonable option is that the verse is referring to Jesus. In this case, we have a multiplied benefit when we pray in tongues – not only does the Holy Spirit intercede on our behalf, but His concern catalytically generates more intercession from Jesus Himself – and we know that the Heavenly Father never denies the requests presented by His Son! (John 15:16, 16:23-27)

One other thing that we need to focus on is that Paul acknowledges that the mysteries that are spoken are from the spirit of the speaker – a concept that might be confusing to some readers because they automatically assume that the tongues come from the Holy Spirit. From the very first occurrence of this phenomenon, the scriptures made it plain that the believers in the Upper

Room on the Day of Pentecost did the speaking as the Holy Spirit gave them the words to say. (Acts 2:4) Thus, speaking in tongues is a joint operation of the inner heart of the believer and the Holy Spirit. As the spirit of the believer cries out for an answer from God, the Holy Spirit takes that request and molds it into the perfect prayer which is then verbalized in tongues by the outward physical being of the believer. As the mystery is unraveled, everything in the believer's life is supernaturally coordinated to work out just right.

Now that we have mentioned the physical and the spiritual dimensions of the believer, we need to also incorporate the soulical nature as well. And Paul does just that in I Corinthians 14:14, "For if I pray in an unknown tongue, my spirit prayeth, but my understanding is unfruitful." The believer's soul is still "out of the loop" at this point. That's why the prayers are considered mysteries – the mind doesn't figure out all the details. But the fact that the mind may still be at a loss doesn't make praying in tongues void or useless. If only we would think for a minute, we'd all realize that major aspects of our lives are controlled by things that don't register as logical in our minds. Let's take love for instance. Can any one of us give a logical, scientific, or mathematical formula or explanation for what happens when a mother sees her baby of the first time or the ongoing love between the parent and the child or what happens when that young man and young woman meet for the first time or how that infatuation turns to affection and matures into a life-long commitment? Of course not, but all of us have committed our lives to that thing called love, whatever it is. In the same way, we can pray mysteries in the spirit and still not have a logical intelligible resolution, but at the same time we will just know everything is all right. It all makes sense in our hearts even if our brains at still at a loss. Paul described this sort of relationship in Ephesians 3:19, "And to know the love of Christ, which passeth knowledge, that ye might be filled with all the fulness of God" – truths which he has referred to as mysteries in verses four and nine of this same chapter. How is it possible to know something that goes beyond knowledge? Obviously, he is expressing the event in which our spirits have experienced the content of the mystery while our brains are still trying to comprehend all the clues. This same message is echoed in I Corinthians 2:9-10, "But as it is written, Eye hath not seen, nor ear heard, neither have entered into the heart of man, the things which God hath prepared for them that love him. But God hath revealed them unto us by his Spirit: for the Spirit searcheth all things, yea, the deep things of God," in which he explains that there are truths and realities that are revealed in the spirit that are still not comprehended by the soulical personality.

Coupled with the gift of speaking in tongues is the gift of prophecy in which the mysteries that the spirit part of the believer has experienced become comprehensible to the intellect, "He that prophesies understands all mysteries." (I Corinthians 13:2) Since the Lord wants our total being to be blessed, He actually advocates that we desire this revelatory gift of prophecy above the other gifts which may only benefit one portion of our personality – for example healing that blesses the physical man or speaking in tongues that can bless the spiritual dimension while leaving the soulical unfulfilled. (I Corinthians 14:1) However, when prophecy comes forth, there is a total blessing that benefits us in every aspect. This is why the apostle stressed that the gathering of believers should focus on prophesy and revelation. (I Corinthians 14:6, 14:26)

Paul stressed that speaking in tongues should be primarily for one's personal use – likely for searching through the mysteries of God – while prophetic exposition of the mysteries of God should be the focal point of public ministry. In fact, he concluded that five words spoken intelligently are better than ten thousand words uttered in an unknown tongue. (I Corinthians 14:19) We can garner two significant thoughts from this summary statement. Considering that the average adult American male typically speaks ten thousand words per day, Paul's reference to this number of words in an unknown tongue emphasizes the point that quantity does not outweigh quality. But the real significance of this statement is found in his positive evaluation of the ability to communicate viable truth succinctly in just five words. In fact, this is exactly the quality that has made Saul of Trasus into Paul the apostle whose writings have changed the world. All you need to do is visit a few Bible colleges and seminaries and take a tour through the libraries that a filled with shelf after shelf of books trying to explain Paul's thirteen short letters. Some of the greatest minds of the past two millennia have spent endless hours and filled uncountable books in their attempt to unpack all the godly mysteries that he exposed in his handful of writings – essentially five words in comparison to the volumes of revelation that have been deducted from them.

Let's take a quick look through some of Paul's statements to see if we can confirm the hypothesis that we have drawn so far. In I Corinthians 4:5, he wrote that we should never judge anything before the time – "until the Lord come, who both will bring to light the hidden things of darkness, and will make manifest the counsels of the hearts: and then shall every man have praise of God." Obviously, he is not referring to the Second Coming of Christ since that would leave every decision hanging until the end of time. Therefore, it is apparent that he is referencing the fact that the Lord can come in each present situation and make His will known. One likely example of this sort of divine intervention was in relationship to Paul's own ordination. In Acts 13:2, the Holy Spirit spoke and directed the elders in Antioch to anoint Paul and Barnabas for the mission work that they were to venture into. This directive came after these church leaders had spent some time in fasting and "ministering to the Lord." Is it possible that this ministry to the Lord was prayer in tongues? (I Corinthians 2:7, 14:2, 14:28) If so, this example can illustrate how we can invite the Lord to manifest Himself and give divine wisdom in matters that need supernatural direction.

The seventh chapter of I Corinthians reveals some interesting levels of confidence concerning the apostle's certainty in the advice that he is rendering in response to the questions that the church had raised concerning marriage. In verse six, he said, "I speak this by permission, and not of commandment." Apparently, he was convinced that his counsel was worthy of acceptance even though he couldn't attribute it one hundred percent to God as a verbatim directive. However, in verse ten, he wrote, "I command, yet not I, but the Lord." This time, he was unquestionable that the counsel he was giving was not his own thought, but the very edict of God. Contrast that with his evaluation of his advice in verse twelve, "But to the rest speak I, not the Lord." Here, the apostle readily admitted that this statement was his own and he was not going to "pull any punches" to try make it look as if he had a word from God on the matter. In verse twenty-five, he again confessed that his guidance was solely his own, "I have no commandment of the Lord: yet I give my judgment, as one that hath obtained mercy of the Lord to be faithful." Finally, in verse forty, he conceded that he was fairly confident that his counsel was in direct accordance with the mind of the Holy Spirit even though he wasn't certain, "I think also that I have the Spirit of God."

In comparison, Paul wrote with unequivocal assurance that he was hearing from the Holy Spirit in I Timothy 4:1, "Now the Spirit speaketh expressly." Even though this is the introductory statement to a new section in the epistle, if we view it as part of the entire letter we will recognize that it transitions from the concluding verse of the previous chapter in which Paul speaks of the mystery of godliness. In this perspective, we can see that the understanding of the mystery and the express message from the Holy Spirit can be seen as companion concepts. In such case, would it be too much of a leap of logic to assume that there could have been an element of revelation that came through Holy Spirit-directed prayer in tongues?

Paul made other references to the fact that the Holy Spirt bore witness to realities in his life. (Romans 1:9, 8:16) Additionally, he claimed that he received revelation directly from the Lord. (I Corinthians 11:23, Galatians 1:12) Perhaps this was his way of saying that his revelations were confirmed in the mouths of two or three witnesses (II Corinthians 13:1) – the Holy Spirit speaking the mind of the Father and the Son (John 16:13-16). Knowing how life-changing the revelations that he had received from the Holy Spirit were in his own life, Paul's most powerful prayer for the church was that they would also be transformed by this same divine revelation.

> *[I] Cease not to give thanks for you, making mention of you in my prayers; That the God of our Lord Jesus Christ, the Father of glory, may give unto you the spirit of wisdom and revelation in the knowledge of him: The eyes of your understanding being enlightened; that ye may know what is the hope of his calling, and what the riches of the glory of his inheritance in the saints." (Ephesians 1:16-18)*

But he doesn't stop with his own intercession, he directs us that we should also pursue the practice of Holy Spirit-empowered prayers, "And take...the sword of the Spirit, which is the word of God: Praying always with all prayer and supplication in the Spirit, and watching thereunto with all perseverance and supplication for all saints." (Ephesians 6:17-18)   Notice the apparently intentional correlation with the Word of God and praying in the Spirit.   It seems likely that Paul received his understanding of the Word of God – and the ability to actually pen words that would become recognized as the very Word of God – through praying in the Holy Spirit; therefore, he admonished the believers that he was discipling to pursue their spiritual connection with divine revelation through prayer in the Spirit.   In I Corinthians 14:15, Paul made the determination that he would purposely pray in the Spirit as well as in the understanding. It is likely this is a reference to the practice of praying mysteries to God in tongues and prophesying the revelations back in an understandable language – the practice that changed him from Saul of Tarsus to Paul the apostle and the practice that can change us from average individuals to men and women whose lives are a present-day manifestation of the Holy Spirit.

> *But the manifestation of the Spirit is given to every man to profit withal. (I Corinthians 12:7)*

Books by Delron & Peggy Shirley

available at www.teachallnationsmission.com

Bingo, a Fresh Look at Grace
Christmas Thoughts
Cornerstones of Faith
Daily Bible Study Series (Five-Volume Set)
Daily Ditties from Delron's Desk (Six Volumes Available)
Dr. Livingstone, I Presume
The Great Commission – Doable
Finally, My Brethren
Going Deeper in Jesus
In This Sign Conquer
Interface
Israel, Key to Human Destiny
Lessons Along the Way
Lessons from the Life of David
Living for the End Times
Maturing into the Full Stature of Jesus Christ
Maximum Impact
Of Kings and Prophets
Passion for the Harvest
People Who Make A Difference
Positioned for Blessing and Power
Problem People of the Bible
Seeds and Harvest
So Send I You
So, You Wanna be a Preacher
The IN Factors
The Last Enemy
The Non-Conformer's Trilogy
Tread Marks
Verse for the Day (Two Volumes Available)
Women for the Harvest
You'll be Darned to Heck if You Don't Believe in Gosh
Your Home Can Survive in the 21st Century

CPSIA information can be obtained
at www.ICGtesting.com
Printed in the USA
FSHW020044081119
63804FS